CELEBRATION GAMES

Physical Activities for Every Month

Barb Wnek, MEd

Human Kinetics

Library of Congress Cataloging-in-Publication Data

Wnek, Barbara, 1949-
  Celebration games : physical activities for every month / Barbara Wnek.
      p. cm.
  "This book is a revised edition of Holiday Games and Activities, published in 1992 by Human Kinetics."
  ISBN 0-7360-5955-5 (soft cover)
  1. Physical fitness for children--Study and teaching (Elementary)--United States. 2. Games--United States. 3. Holidays--United States. I. Wnek, Barbara, 1949- Holiday games and activities. II. Title.
  GV443.W57 2006
  372.86--dc22

                                        2005028831

ISBN-10: 0-7360-5955-5
ISBN-13: 978-0-7360-5955-8

This book is a revised edition of *Holiday Games and Activities,* published in 1992 by Human Kinetics, Inc.

Acquisitions Editor: Bonnie Pettifor; **Managing Editor:** Kathleen D. Bernard; **Copyeditor:** Amy Kahrliker; **Proofreader:** John Wentworth; **Permission Manager:** Dalene Reeder; **Graphic Designer:** Fred Starbird; **Graphic Artist:** Denise Lowry; **Cover Designer:** Keith Blomberg; **Photographer (cover and interior):** Sarah Ritz; **Illustrators:** Tim Offenstein and Kelly Hendren; **Printer:** Versa Press

We thank the St. Louis Charter School in St. Louis, Missouri, for assistance in providing the location for the photo shoot for this book.

Printed in the United States of America   10   9   8   7   6   5   4   3   2   1

Human Kinetics
Web site: www.HumanKinetics.com

United States: Human Kinetics, P.O. Box 5076, Champaign, IL 61825-5076
800-747-4457
e-mail: humank@hkusa.com

Canada: Human Kinetics, 475 Devonshire Road Unit 100, Windsor, ON N8Y 2L5
800-465-7301 (in Canada only)
e-mail: orders@hkcanada.com

Europe: Human Kinetics, 107 Bradford Road, Stanningley, Leeds LS28 6AT
United Kingdom
+44 (0) 113 255 5665
e-mail: hk@hkeurope.com

Australia: Human Kinetics, 57A Price Avenue, Lower Mitcham, South Australia 5062
08 8277 1555
e-mail: liaw@hkaustralia.com

New Zealand: Human Kinetics, Division of Sports Distributors NZ Ltd.
P.O. Box 300 226 Albany, North Shore City, Auckland
0064 9 448 1207
e-mail: info@humankinetics.co.nz

To everyone who lets me express my enthusiasm and creativity.
And to all of my students, who learn and have fun
through these activities.
And Mom, here's another one just for you!

CONTENTS

PREFACE

Never say never. Many years ago I said I would never write another book because of all the work involved. I also said I would never run another marathon after my first one. Well, 40 marathons later, I've written another book. I've had so much fun motivating my physical education and health students with dancing fruits and vegetables, skeletons, cows, giant milk cartons, and music that I wanted to tell other educators about these ideas. I've read that running and other aerobic activities enhance creativity. It's been true for me: Here's my second book, *Celebration Games*.

A student I taught many years ago made my day when she recognized me recently. She is 19 now. We started reminiscing, and she said she didn't remember any other teachers' names; she just remembered mine. She kept repeating that I was the only one she remembered because of all the fun activities we did.

The school year is filled with holidays. This book presents physical fitness activities, skills, games, and rhythm and dance activities for kindergarten through sixth grade, in a holiday or seasonal theme. Most of the activities can easily be adapted for various grade or skill levels and can fit into any curriculum. There are even ideas for school-wide family events.

Activities become special depending on the equipment used. My inventor friend, Gary Kellman, gives me all kinds of things such as rubber stars, hearts, sport balls, tubes, and caps to incorporate into my games. You can find a variety of things to use at recycling centers. People discard some really good stuff! Even old activities take on a new look with different equipment.

I'm always thinking of new activities, like the Health Bee. It is my own creation, which motivates my students all year long to study hard in health class. I have students following me around school begging me to be fruits and vegetables for the Bee. Planning the entertainment and music is so much fun, too.

I also thought of the strobe light activities that make everyone lose inhibitions. Shyness disappears when the strobes are flashing and the children's shadows appear on the walls.

The preparation for some of these activities may take a few extra minutes, but it is well worth it. Be sure to read "How to Use This Book" so you will be able to present the activities as effectively as possible. The activities will bring excitement to your physical education classes, motivate your students, and provide enjoyable educational experiences. Have fun!

ACKNOWLEDGMENTS

First, I would like to thank the thousands of children, especially those at Commons Lane Elementary School, Halls Ferry Elementary School, and Parker Road Elementary School in the Ferguson-Florissant School District, who continue to inspire me to create activities like the ones in this book. I'd also like to thank my principals, Dr. Barbara Wright, Mrs. Lisa Hazel, and Mrs. Sharon Norvell. Special thanks go to Susan C. Flesch, program director of the Gifted Resource Council, where I have taught gifted and talented children for 19 summers. A huge thanks goes to the following people, who have helped me in some special way to make my activities the best they can be:

Amy Myrdal, Dole 5 A Day (prizes and educational materials)

Mike O'Brien, vice president of produce for Schnucks Markets (prizes)

Fresh Express Fresh Foods (prizes)

Gary Kellman, inventor (equipment)

Frank Cale, Dole Foods (Bobby Banana)

Marta Maitles and John Heidkamp, Dole Fresh Fruit

Gene Bollefer, librarian at Commons Lane School (computer help and videotaping)

Anne Welty, computer wizard at Commons Lane School (computer help)

Doug Wright, teacher at Commons Lane School (music)

Dr. Tom Loughrey, University of Missouri at St. Louis

Emily Price, St. Louis Dairy Council (educational materials and displays)

Diane Baklor and Linda Hemmerla, Remember Me Vintage Clothing (costumes)

St. Louis Trophy and Engraving Company

Tracy Garrett, A.J. Waide, and student models, St. Louis Charter School

Chuck Rebeck (educational displays)

Walter Wnek, my brother (computer advice)

Chris McQueen at Ice Cream Specialties

Finally, thanks to Human Kinetics and Bonnie Pettifor, Kathleen Bernard, and Sarah Ritz for helping me make this book a reality.

HOW TO USE THIS BOOK

Please take a few minutes to read the information that follows so that you can use the games and activities to motivate and excite your students.

How the Book Is Organized

The book is divided thematically into eight chapters that encompass the seasons and holidays of the school year, beginning with August and September and ending with May, June, and July. December and January are also combined to include the winter and holiday season. Each chapter contains all or some of the following activities:

- Skills practice stations
- Games, including chasing and fleeing games, cooperative games, relays, and fitness games
- Rhythm and dance activities
- Obstacle courses with award certificates
- School-wide family activities
- Ideas for designing bulletin boards
- Holiday information
- Materials and resources for activities
- Exercise circuit training course with seasonal awards

The explanations for each of the activities are given in a format that shows at a glance the important things you need to know in order to present the activity to your class. Many activities include an explanatory photograph. The following information is presented for each activity:

- The activity title gives the activity a fun name to create excitement among the students.
- A quick description summarizes the activity.
- The section on appropriate ages tells what ages the activity is most successful with.

- Activity goals describe intended outcomes of the activities for the students.
- The space required section tells what type of space is most suitable for the activity.
- The key skills section shows what skills are emphasized in the activity.
- The equipment and preparation section describes the equipment needed for the activity and explains any activity preparation that might be necessary.
- The activity procedure explains how to conduct the activity and includes suggestions to make it proceed smoothly. See the next section for more complete information on procedures for skills stations and obstacle courses.
- Safety considerations alert you to potential safety concerns specific to each activity.
- Adaptation suggestions present ideas about how the activity may be used in various situations.

How to Use the Appendix

The appendix includes patterns for materials used in some of the activities. You can reproduce these materials as needed. It also includes narratives about some of the holidays.

How to Structure Classes

You can use the activities individually, or you can combine them to encompass an entire class period. You should precede the activities with a warm-up, and then one or more of the games or rhythmic activities could follow. Station activities probably take an entire period. Motivational activities for fitness should be ongoing. The ages, skill levels, and needs of your students will determine the amount of time necessary for each activity.

Procedure for Skills Stations and Obstacle Courses

The following is the groundwork for all games where the students participate at skill stations or in obstacle courses.

Skills Stations

The procedures for conducting the skills stations are basically the same for each season. The following information should make the skills stations run smoothly.

Divide the class evenly among the stations. Have students draw numbers out of a hat and then put the students in numerical order to prevent arguments about who is first. Tell them to keep this order for all of the stations, which are also in numerical order. Designate the number of tries that each student may take each time his or her turn comes up. The first student in each group takes a turn. The second student in each group takes a turn, and so on. Students continue to take turns until you give them the signal to stop. Students clean up their stations for the next group. Make sure the equipment remains at its station. Each group then rotates to the next station. The student taking a turn when the stop signal is given becomes the first turn-taker at the next station. The other students line up in numerical order behind that student. With this method, everyone gets an equal number of turns. Give the stop signal when you see that all of the students have had at least one turn at their stations. The students may keep score at the skills stations if desired. Leave ample space between the stations and ensure that students waiting their turns keep a safe distance from the performers.

Station work is a good opportunity to give individual help, but watch for students who have difficulty staying on task. Some students need more time to adjust to the freedom involved in station work.

Obstacle Courses

Divide the class into as many groups as there are activities in the obstacle course. Start each group at a different activity. Pair up students so that one of the pair participates in the course while the other watches to ensure that the skills are being performed correctly and to count the number of obstacles touched. The first group of students starts on your signal. When these students finish the course, they should be back at their starting point. Partners then change places and wait for the signal. The remainder of the class performs the obstacle course in the same manner.

Emphasize that the obstacle course is not a race; accidents happen when children rush through activities. Stress correct form when avoiding obstacles. Keeping some space between the students is important for safety and for allowing each student to perform well. If a traffic jam occurs, have students wait patiently. Spread the obstacle course out as much as possible. Review safety rules for scooterboards. Keep scooterboards under control at all times. To prevent injuries, make sure you place an adequate number of mats around equipment such as the balance beam, horizontal ladder, ropes, and cargo net.

Keep in mind the title of the book: *Celebration Games*. Your students will have fun learning to live healthy and active lifestyles through these activities. You can always find a reason to celebrate!

AUGUST AND SEPTEMBER

Back to School

START—AND STAY—ON THE RIGHT FOOT

Quick Description

Physical fitness exercise circuit training course with seasonal awards (see pages 141-148)

Appropriate Ages

5 to 12

Activity Goals

To improve physical fitness levels, especially muscular strength, muscular endurance, flexibility, and cardiovascular endurance, by motivating the students to put more effort into the physical fitness exercises

Space Required

Gymnasium, track, or large outdoor area

Key Skills

A circuit training course can emphasize the following skills:

- Arm and shoulder strength and endurance
- Abdominal strength

- Leg strength and endurance
- Flexibility
- Cardiovascular endurance

Equipment and Preparation

Choose the exercises from the list that follows, or substitute your own, and teach students how to perform them correctly. Remember to alternate the major muscle groups being exercised. Make signs for each exercise or use dry-erase boards. Put up a picture of each exercise, or take photographs of students performing the exercises correctly and use those. Set up the signs and any equipment needed for the exercises. Play seasonal music. Reproduce the seasonal awards for your students.

A student does arm curls at the August and September fitness station.

Activity Procedure

1. Divide the class evenly among the stations.
2. When you give the signal, have students perform the exercise at the station for as long as they can. Allow 10 to 20 seconds at each station. When the time limit is up for the first station, blow a whistle. This is the signal for students to change stations.
3. The students jog or perform another locomotor skill for one complete lap, move counterclockwise, pass the station they just completed, and proceed to the next station. Then they perform the exercise at that station until the whistle blows for them to jog another lap.

This procedure continues until students have performed all of the exercises, jogged all of the laps, and are back to their starting stations. Students earn a seasonal certificate for completing the course a specified number of times in a given time period, such as a week or two.

Safety Considerations

Emphasize correct form while the students are performing the exercises. Tell them to jog at an even pace and not to race when it is time to change stations. Also, tell them to return any equipment to its place, away from the jogging area.

Adaptation Suggestions

Choose exercises according to your students' needs and abilities. Here are some suggestions:

Arm and Shoulder Strength and Endurance

1. Alternate arm curls with hand weights
2. Overhead shoulder press with hand weights
3. Arm circles
4. Push-ups or modified push-ups
5. Crab kicks
6. Wall push-ups
7. Modified pull-ups on bar
8. Exercises with exercise bands, such as arm curls or shoulder press
9. Pull-ups or flexed-arm hang

Abdominal Strength and Endurance

1. Bent-knee curl-ups with hands at sides or crossed on chest
2. Bicycle pedaling
3. Reverse sit-ups

Leg Strength and Endurance

1. Skier's wall sit
2. Side leg lifts
3. Alternate elbow-to-knee touches
4. Crab kicks
5. Mountain climbers

Flexibility

1. Straddle stretch
2. Hurdle stretch
3. Straight-leg stretch
4. Triceps stretch
5. Trunk stretch

Cardiovascular Endurance

1. Rope jumping
2. Step aerobics
3. Jumping jacks

NUTRITION SKILLS STATIONS

Quick Description

Throwing, kicking, jumping, hopping, and strengthening stations

Appropriate Ages

5 to 12

Activity Goals

To improve knowledge of nutrition and to develop throwing and kicking skills

Space Required

Gymnasium

Key Skills

Underhand and overhand throwing, kicking, jumping, hopping, and strengthening

Equipment and Preparation

Make a sign for each station and organize the following equipment:

1. A-spar-a-gus—Bowling pins and balls
2. Tic-tac-to-matoes—Red beanbags and tic-tac-toe outline with tape on floor
3. Salad Bar—Pull-up bars or other climbing bars

While doing pull-ups at the Salad Bar fitness station, students are reminded that a healthy diet includes five or more servings of fruit and vegetables.

4. Say "Cheese"—Picture of a smiley face and small yarn or foam balls
5. Carrot Kicks—Bowling pins and foam soccer balls
6. Potato Pass—Footballs
7. Balanced Diet—Spoons, plastic eggs, and low balance beam
8. Bread Basket—Plastic tubs or baskets and beanbags or balls
9. Junk-Food Jungle Jumps—Poly spots (flat, rubber shapes to place on the floor as markers during activities) with pictures of junk foods on them
10. Chicken Challenge—Tape line on floor

Activity Procedure

Review the activity procedures for skills stations on pages xii to xiii. Explain each station to the class.

Station Description

1. A-spar-a-gus—Students roll balls at the bowling pins.
2. Tic-tac-to-matoes—Students toss beanbags onto the tic-tac-toe board, trying to fill three squares in a row.
3. Salad Bar—Students perform pull-ups or flexed-arm hangs or climb the wall climber.
4. Say "Cheese"—Students throw beanbags or balls at the smiley-face mouth.
5. Carrot Kicks—Students kick foam soccer balls at the bowling pins.
6. Potato Pass—Students throw a football back and forth to a partner, counting the number of throws until they miss.
7. Balanced Diet—Students travel across a balance beam while balancing a plastic egg on a spoon.
8. Bread Basket—Students throw beanbags or balls into the tubs or baskets.
9. Junk-Food Jungle Jumps—Students jump over as many of the poly spots as they can, avoiding the junk foods.
10. Chicken Challenge—Students hop as many times as possible over a line, first on the right foot and then on the left foot.

Safety Considerations

Tell students to be careful when changing stations and to put the equipment in the correct place so no one trips on it.

Adaptation Suggestions

The distances can be adjusted for different ages and skill levels.

THE ROAD OF RULES

Quick Description

Obstacle course

Appropriate Ages

5 to 12

Activity Goals

To complete the skills in the obstacle course correctly while cooperating with a partner and to learn the physical education positive behavior rules of safety, respect, cooperation, peacefulness, kindness, and responsibility

Students cooperate to maneuver the scooterboard through the positive behavior road signs.

Space Required

Gymnasium

Key Skills

Cooperation and control in maneuvering a partner on a scooterboard through obstacles; knowledge of class rules

Equipment and Preparation

Construct signs or use dry-erase boards that resemble traffic signs. The signs can say the following phrases:

- Be safe
- Be respectful
- Be cooperative
- Be peaceful
- Be kind
- Be responsible

Set up the course to resemble a street with obstacles through which students can maneuver the scooterboards. You will need one scooterboard for every two students.

Activity Procedure

1. Review the activity procedures for obstacle courses on page xiii.
2. Pair off students and explain the obstacle course to the class.
3. One student is the driver and the other is the passenger. The passenger sits on the scooterboard with legs crossed and not touching the floor, while the other student pushes him or her through the course.
4. As the students pass the various positive behavior signs, the passenger tells the driver two examples of that rule that pertains to physical education class.

The following could be used as examples:

- Be safe: Don't chew gum. Watch out for other people.
- Be respectful: Be a good listener. Use appropriate language.
- Be cooperative: Work nicely with other students and take turns. Follow game rules.

- Be kind: Don't laugh at other students. Make sure to include others in your activities.
- Be peaceful: Don't argue or fight.
- Be responsible: Take good care of equipment. Be honest.

After traveling through the course, the driver and passenger change roles, and they follow the same procedure.

Safety Considerations

Emphasize the importance of scooterboard safety to the students and explain that the course is not a race.

Adaptation Suggestions

Arrange the course according to the abilities of the students. If younger students are having trouble pushing someone on a scooter, then one can ride it and the other can walk beside to hear the rules.

FOOD GUIDE AND ACTIVITY PYRAMID RELAY

Quick Description

Students retrieve pictures of various foods and physical activities and place them on the correct area of the MyPyramid.

Appropriate Ages

5 to 12

Activity Goals

To place the food and activity pictures in the correct area on the accompanying pyramid

Space Required

Gymnasium

Key Skills

Running; knowledge of current dietary and activity guidelines.

Equipment and Preparation

Obtain pictures of a variety of foods from food labels or packages, and also obtain pictures of people doing various physical activities. You will need six or more outlines of the MyPyramid illustration and activity pyramid, either on large paper or taped to the floor.

Activity Procedure

1. Divide the class as evenly as possible into six or more lines. Have each line sit behind one of the pyramid outlines.

2. At the other end of the playing area, spread out the food and activity pictures.

3. On the signal, the first student in each row runs to the food pictures, brings one back, and places it in the correct area of the pyramid. Then the next student runs and retrieves a picture. This continues until all pictures have been retrieved.

4. Count the number of pictures placed in the correct places on the pyramid.

5. Talk about the number of servings students should eat each day from the food groups and the amount of physical activity they should be doing.

Safety Considerations

Tell students to be careful not to slip on the pieces.

Adaptation Suggestions

Put up a large poster of the pyramids for the younger students to follow when they do this activity.

"BEE" A GOOD CITIZEN TAG GAME

Quick Description

A chasing and fleeing game to reinforce positive behaviors

Appropriate Ages

5 to 9

Positive behaviors are reinforced by students as they repeat the "Bee" phrases.

Activity Goals

To demonstrate bodily control, knowledge of the game, and safety rules in a game situation; to give examples of positive behaviors

Space Required

Gymnasium or outdoor area

Key Skills

Running, dodging, and tagging safely; knowledge of positive behaviors

Equipment and Preparation

Use three or four "Bees," depending on the size of your class. Bumblebee beanbags work well for this game. You can find stuffed toy bees at most discount stores or make paper ones and laminate them (see page 149).

Activity Procedure

1. Choose three or four students to be chasers, and give each of them one of the bees.
2. Have each chaser say one of the "Bee" phrases, which are "be safe," "be respectful," "be cooperative," "be peaceful," "be kind," and "be responsible." When the chasers tag a student with the bee, the student must freeze and flap his or her arms up and down.
3. Also, choose two or three students to be the "melters." When a melter sees a student flapping his or her arms, the melter goes to him or her; the student must tell the melter an example of one of the "Bee" phrases.
4. After a tagged student has been melted, have the student return to the game.
5. Choose new chasers and melters frequently.

Safety Considerations

Stress to students to watch where they are running, to avoid collisions, and to tag gently—and not on the face or head.

Adaptation Suggestions

The playing area can be made larger or smaller according to the students' abilities.

FRIEND-TO-FRIEND GAME

Quick Description

Getting-to-know-you mixer and memory game involving identifying body parts and coordinating body parts to achieve body positions

Appropriate Ages

5 to 12

Students make new friends and coordinate body parts.

Activity Goals

To give students a chance to meet the students in their class and remember different partners in a game situation

Space Required

Full or half gymnasium

Key Skills

Knowledge of body parts; memory skills

Equipment and Preparation

Students can wear name tags if needed.

Activity Procedure

1. Tell students that each time you call out a body part they must find a partner and get into a position with that partner so that those body parts are touching (e.g., feet to feet, hand to hand, elbow to elbow, or back to back).
2. Call out a new body part. Students must find a new partner and get into the new position.
3. Make the game more difficult by saying, "Right hand to partner's left knee" or "Left thumb to partner's forehead."
4. After a while, repeat the different body part combinations and have the students find the partner that they originally did that body part combination with.

Safety Considerations

Tell students that, in order to avoid collisions, they should be careful when they are changing partners.

Adaptation Considerations

Older students can play using the names of muscles or bones (for example, right hand to left biceps or left hand to skull).

SAFETY FIRST BAND-AID TAG

Quick Description

A chasing and fleeing game

Appropriate Ages

5 to 12

Activity Goals

To demonstrate bodily control and knowledge of game and safety rules in a game situation

Space Required

Gymnasium or outdoor area

Key Skills

Running, chasing, fleeing, dodging, honesty, good sportsmanship, and knowledge of safety procedures

Students learn how to tag safely.

Equipment and Preparation

First-aid posters

Activity Procedure

Discuss safety and first-aid procedures with the students. Choose two or three students to be "it" and two or three more to be the first-aid helpers. Have students scatter in the playing area. When a student is tagged by one of the "its," he or she must cover that body part with his or her hands like a Band-Aid. If the student is tagged again, he or she covers that spot with his or her other hand and continues to play. When the student is tagged for the third time, he or she must freeze and wait for "first aid." When the first-aid helpers touch him or her, he or she is back in the game, injury free, not covering any body parts. Choose new taggers frequently.

Safety Considerations

Stress that students avoid collisions by keeping their heads up while covering body parts.

Adaptation Suggestions

Reduce or enlarge the size of the playing area according to ability and choose more or fewer taggers according to the size of the class.

HEALTH BEE

Quick Description

Demonstration of health and physical education knowledge (for some sample questions, see the end of this activity)

Appropriate Ages

10- to 12-year-olds are competitors and 5- to 9-year-olds are the audience participants and special performers.

Health Bee characters entertain and help students learn health curriculum material.

Sample Score Sheet and Seating Arrangement

Emily Crecelius	Kelly Kuberski	Tyrone Sanders	Andrew Stanley	James Martinez
Lee Matton	Sarah Hill	David Smith	Bianca Gentry	Cory Damien
Aron Gray	Temisha Smith	Kathie Quain	Javier Solis	Katie Jendra

Activity Goals

To instill excitement and enthusiasm for health and physical education

Space Required

Gymnasium

Key Skills

Knowledge of health and physical education information

Equipment and Preparation

1. Compile a list of questions from your health and physical education classes as the Health Bee Test.
2. Give students a study sheet. Those who score high on the test become participants in the Health Bee. The test can also be used as part of the students' health grades.
3. Create additional questions for the Health Bee.
4. Gather a dry-erase board, a dry-erase marker, and a chair for each contestant.
5. Tape index cards with the contestants' names to the chairs so they know where to sit.
6. Ask three or four staff members to be the scorekeepers. The seating arrangement and the score sheets match each other.
7. Consider going to local supermarkets, printing and engraving companies, or corporations with healthy-choice programs (for example, Dole 5 A Day) for donations to use as prizes, trophies, decorations, or for costumes for the entertainers to use.

8. Develop entertainment, such as sketches or songs, according to the questions (see Adaptation Suggestions).

Activity Procedure

Contestants enter the gym and find their chairs. All of the other students and staff enter the gym and sit down, facing the contestants. Explain the Health Bee to the audience and how the contestants were selected. A short bit of entertainment precedes each question to make the Health Bee even more fun. Ask the contestants a question and have them write their answers on the dry-erase boards. On signal, they show their answers to the audience and the scorekeepers. The scorekeepers mark "correct" or "incorrect" on the score sheet for each answer. While the scores are being tabulated, ask the audience a question and give a prize for the correct answer. This continues for about 45 minutes and then winners are selected. The students with the most correct answers are the winners. If students' scores are tied, prepare some more difficult questions or give out more trophies. Every contestant receives a prize. You may want to have someone videotape the program.

Safety Considerations

Keep the performers a safe distance from the audience. Keep cords away from the students or tape the cords down so no one trips on them.

Adaptation Suggestions

You can make the questions as easy or as difficult as you like, according to the abilities of the students.

The following are some sample questions, props, and songs that you can use as part of your own Health Bee. Review the following key first:

Health Bee Questions and Answers—HBQ and A

Entertainment—ENT

Audience Questions and Answers—AQ and A

HBQ: What leg bone is connected to your pelvis?

A: Femur

ENT: Elvis the Pelvis and the Bone Brothers dance around to the Elvis Presley song *All Shook Up*. One student wears an Elvis costume, and three students wear skeleton costumes.

AQ: What is another name for the pelvis?

A: Hip bone

HBQ: What body system moves food through your body?

A: Digestive system

ENT: The Salad Sisters (our cafeteria ladies) dance and push the salad bar cart to the Dole 5 A Day song "The Salad Sisters."

AQ: What doesn't contain any nutrients but helps move food through your body?

A: Fiber

HBQ: What type of exercise is a sit-up?

A: Anaerobic

ENT: Muscle Boy, a student wearing a T-shirt with the muscles on it, flexes his muscles for the audience, and then demonstrates sit-ups.

AQ: What muscles are you using when you do sit-ups?

A: Abdominal

HBQ: What does toothpaste contain that helps prevent cavities?

A: Fluoride

ENT: A student "Tooth Fairy," wearing wings and carrying a giant toothbrush that I made, "flies" around to the theme music of *Star Wars*.

AQ: What should you do to your teeth every day besides brushing?

A: Floss

HBQ: What does SPF stand for?

A: Sun protection factor

ENT: I chose a teacher from the audience, sat her down in a lawn chair, and put a large sun hat and very large clown sunglasses on her. A student held an inflatable sunshine face above her. Another student carried in a giant sun screen bottle that I made with SPF on it. I played the old song *Here Comes Summer.*

AQ: What disease can you get from too much sun?

A: Skin cancer

HBQ: What mineral does milk give you to make your bones strong?

A: Calcium

ENT: Two students dressed as cows and one as a giant milk carton skipped around to the Dairy Council's song *Moo to You.*

AQ: What is taken out of the milk if it is labeled skim milk?

A: Fat

Other Props

- Giant plastic egg—You can find them at Easter time.
- Inflatable eyeballs—You can find them in the Oriental Trading Company catalogue.
- Inflatable fish—You can find them where they sell swimming pool toys.
- Plastic bones—You can find them at Halloween time

Music

- The Dole Food Company has a free cassette of 5 A Day songs, such as "5 A DAY," "B is for Banana," "Salad Sisters," "Vitamin C," and "Fiber." Find out more at www.Dole5ADay.com.

Other Songs

- "Heat Wave," by Martha and the Vandellas—Ask a question about hyperthermia.
- "Rescue Me," by Fontella Bass—Ask questions about first aid.
- "Candy Man," by Sammy Davis Jr.—Ask questions about junk food.
- "1-2-3," by Len Barry—Ask questions about the benefits of dairy products.
- "I Feel Good," by James Brown—A student who acts as a James Brown impersonator is asked how he feels when he eats well, exercises, gets enough sleep, and doesn't smoke or do drugs. Of course the answer is "I Feel Good."

OCTOBER

Halloween

Quick Description

Ball handling, striking, and kicking skills stations

Appropriate Ages

5 to 12

Activity Goals

To improve form and accuracy while rolling, underhand throwing, overhand throwing, striking with a bat, and kicking

Space Required

Gymnasium

Key Skills

Rolling, underhand throwing, overhand throwing, striking with a bat, and kicking

Equipment and Preparation

Make a sign for each station and organize the following equipment:

1. Ghost Throwing—Make three handkerchief ghosts and obtain a container such as a box or trash can to use as the target.

Students name the bone they are throwing the ball at while playing at the Rattle the Bones station.

2. Monster Mouth—Make a picture of a scary mouth on a sheet of paper or cut out a mouth on a cardboard box; gather three beanbags.
3. Soccer Ghoul—Make a soccer "ghoul" by attaching a ghoul or ghost picture to two traffic cones or indoor soccer goals. Obtain three foam soccer balls.
4. Ghost Getters—Draw a ghost on three empty plastic milk bottles or white bowling pins. Obtain three beanbags or lightweight balls.
5. Fill the Treat Basket—Turn a large traffic cone upside down and cover it with black paper. Obtain three beanbags or small balls.

6. Rattle the Bones—Find a large picture of a skeleton and obtain three beanbags.

7. I'm Bats About Halloween—Use a batting tee, a plastic bat, and three lightweight balls.

Set up the stations in the gym and attach the corresponding signs to the wall. Mark the floor with tape which students must stand behind while waiting for their turns.

Activity Procedure

Review the activity procedures for skills stations on pages xii to xiii. Explain each station to the class. Allow each student three attempts at each station to avoid confusion.

Station Descriptions

1. Ghost Throwing—Students throw the "ghosts" into the containers.

2. Monster Mouth—Students throw beanbags into the "mouth."

3. Soccer Ghoul—Students kick the soccer ball between the "ghoul posts."

4. Ghost Getters—Students throw beanbags or lightweight balls at the ghosts.

5. Fill the Treat Basket—Students throw beanbags or balls into the cone.

6. Rattle the Bones—Students throw beanbags at the skeleton. They can aim for specified bones.

7. I'm Bats About Halloween—Students hit the lightweight ball off the batting tee.

Safety Considerations

Make sure that students who are waiting their turns are not too close to the student who is taking a turn, especially at the batting-tee station. The student who just finished his or her turn can retrieve the balls or beanbags for the next student. Otherwise too many students will be chasing balls and may cause collisions.

Adaptation Suggestions

The targets can be adapted to any skill level by raising or lowering the targets for rolling and by shortening or lengthening the distances to the targets.

ESCAPE FROM THE SPIDERS

Quick Description

Obstacle course

Appropriate Ages

5 to 12

Activity Goals

To complete the skills in the obstacle course without touching any of the paper spiders

Space Required

Gymnasium

Key Skills

Bodily control while performing the entire obstacle course, perceptual motor skills, hand-eye coordination, foot-eye coordination, agility, and upper body strength.

Students travel through the obstacle course without stepping on the spiders.

Equipment and Preparation

1. Copy and laminate 30 or more paper spiders (see page 150) and enough "I Escaped From the Spiders" certificates (see page 151) for everyone in your class. The certificates are optional.

2. Assemble the obstacle course and attach the paper spiders at various places along the course.

3. Adjust the course according to the equipment available.

4. Some or all of the following will be needed for this activity:
   - Hanging ropes, climbing ladders, horizontal ladders, and cargo nets
   - Four or more rubber bases
   - One parachute draped over chairs to make a tunnel or a tunnel made from mats
   - Five or more traffic cones
   - Enough mats to use under and around the equipment

5. To create excitement and interest, put up signs that say "The Spiders Are Coming! Will You Be Able to Escape?" around the school about a week before the activity is scheduled.

Activity Procedure

Review the obstacle course procedures on page xiii. Explain the obstacle course to the class. Students who complete the course receive an "I Escaped From the Spiders" certificate.

The following activities are included in the sample course:

- Hanging Rope Challenge—Travel along the ropes without falling into the spider pit.
- Base Jumping—Jump from base to base without stepping on the spiders on the floor.
- Monkey Bars—Travel along the rungs of the horizontal ladder without falling into the spider pit.
- Deep Dark Tunnel—Crawl through the tunnel without touching any spiders.
- Spider's Web—Climb up and down the spider's web (cargo net) without touching any spiders.
- Obstacle Challenge—Climb over ladders or obstacles without touching any spiders.

Safety Considerations

Stress safety on all of the equipment and emphasize that the obstacle course is not a race.

Adaptation Suggestions

Vary the activities according to the abilities of the students, such as adding more spiders to make it more difficult to avoid them.

TRICK-OR-TREAT TAG

Quick Description

A chasing and fleeing game in which students try to steal the Halloween treats that are being guarded by monsters

Appropriate Ages

5 to 12

Activity Goals

To demonstrate bodily control and knowledge of game and safety rules in a game situation

Space Required

Gymnasium

Key Skills

Running, chasing, fleeing, dodging and tagging safely; developing honesty and good sportsmanship

Equipment and Preparation

1. Spread out a large number, 50 or more, of beanbags or other objects, such as craft sticks, across the floor at one end of the length of the gym.
2. Place a cone at the other end of the gym for each line to sit behind.
3. Stand one mat up on each side of the width of the gym. One is the monster's dungeon and the other is the rescuer's house.
4. Using other mats, make a tunnel on the rescuer's side.

A student steals treats while the monster is about to tag and send another student to the dungeon.

Activity Procedure

1. Divide the class as evenly as possible into about eight lines. (The number of lines will be the number of students running across the gym at the same time. Too many would not be safe.)

2. Choose two students to be monsters and two students to be rescuers. Designate them with different-colored jerseys.

3. Have the two monsters guard the Halloween treats.

4. Tell the first student in each row to run and steal a treat.

5. If the monster tags him or her, he or she must go to the dungeon.

6. If the student gets tagged with a treat in his or her hand, the

student must return it to the pile of treats before going to the dungeon.

7. If the student is successful in stealing the treat, he or she puts it under his or her team's cone.

8. When a rescuer sees students in the dungeon, he or she must cross the width of the gym to rescue one student at a time by holding hands.

9. If they make it back safely to the rescuer's house, the student crawls through the haunted tunnel to return to his or her line.

10. If the monster tags the student while being rescued, he or she must go back to the dungeon.

11. Rescuers can't be tagged.

12. Change monsters and rescuers frequently.

Safety Considerations

Students will be running the length and width of the gym. Emphasize extra safety when running and when crawling through the tunnel.

Adaptation Suggestions

If students are always getting tagged and not returning with any treats, let them steal two pieces and return only one if they get tagged. That way they will always bring one piece back.

SPIDERS IN THE WEB

Quick Description

Students throw beanbags, plastic spiders, poker chips, or other small items that won't bounce too far, into the plastic or paper spider web.

Appropriate Ages

5 to 10

Activity Goals

To improve throwing for accuracy

Space Required

Full or half gym

A student practices throwing skills to fill the web with spiders.

Key Skills

Underhand and overhand throwing

Equipment and Preparation

1. Purchase plastic Halloween tablecloths from a large discount department store at Halloween time. They will last a long time. Or, make your own from paper.
2. Purchase small plastic or rubber spiders to throw into the spider webs, or use other objects to fill the web.
3. Obtain a few containers to hold the spiders.

Activity Procedure

1. Divide the class as evenly as possible into lines according to how many spider webs you have. Two lines can aim at the same spider web.
2. Place a container of spiders between each row and a short distance away from the spider webs.
3. Have the first student in each line run to the container, take out one spider, and throw it toward the spider web. If the spider

lands in the web, it stays there. If it lands on the floor, the student returns it to the container.

4. This procedure continues as long as you like.

5. Use a large number of spiders so that the game can continue without having to remove them from the spider web.

Safety Considerations

Tell students not to walk on the spider webs because they are slippery.

Adaptation Suggestions

The throwing distance to the spider web can be adjusted according to ability.

PUMPKIN-FACE BALL ACTIVITIES

Quick Description

Students practice ball-handling skills and play games using the pumpkin-face balls.

Appropriate Ages

5 to 9

Activity Goals

To improve rolling, bouncing, throwing, and catching skills

Space Required

Full or half gymnasium

Key Skills

Rolling, bouncing, underhand and overhand throwing, catching, and listening

Equipment and Preparation

1. Find orange pumpkin-face playground balls at a large discount department store at Halloween time. You could also draw pumpkin faces on orange playground balls with a black marker.

Pumpkins and students smile while jumping.

2. Buckets can be used to hold each ball; orange and black ones would keep with the theme. Use two orange cones for each line.

3. Place one bucket and ball halfway across the gym and a cone at each end of the gym.

Note: Fun equipment makes the activities more exciting. Set up all of the smiling pumpkin-face balls in a row so when the students enter the gym, they start smiling, too.

Activity Procedure

1. Divide the class as evenly as possible into the same number of lines as you have pumpkin balls and cones.

2. Have each group of students sit behind a cone at one end of the gym.

3. Give the students the following directions:
   - Skip to the bucket
   - Throw the ball up and catch it five times.
   - Walk and dribble the ball around the orange cone and back to the bucket.
   - Place the ball in the bucket and skip back to your line.
   - Go to the end of the line.
4. Tell the next student to begin.
5. Have the students stop when everyone in their row has had a turn.
6. Then give them new directions.

Any activity you do using playground balls becomes so much more fun at Halloween time by using pumpkin-face balls.

Safety Considerations

Tell the students to watch where they are moving so they don't trip over the cones.

Adaptation Suggestions

Make the skills any degree of difficulty you want.

PEDOMETERS IN THE PUMPKIN PATCH

Quick Description

Students use pedometer skills and running or walking in the plastic pumpkin patch to figure out a secret message.

Appropriate Ages

5 to 12

Activity Goals

To learn and reinforce pedometer skills; to run or walk for exercise

Space Required

Use a large outdoor or indoor area. A larger area results in more exercise.

Students record the number of steps they take in the pumpkin patch.

Key Skills

Walking, running, reading a pedometer, and listening

Equipment and Preparation

1. Obtain at least twelve plastic pumpkins, depending on the secret message.

2. Put a few pencils in each pumpkin.

3. Create a simple "secret" message (for example, "Healthy Halloween").

4. Obtain enough index cards to put one letter from the secret message on each index card.

5. Turn the cards over and number them.

6. Attach the index cards, numbered sides up, to each pumpkin.

7. Randomly spread the pumpkins out on the playing "field" (indoors or outdoors).

8. Gather a pedometer and record sheet (see page 152) for each student.

Activity Procedure

1. Teach students the basics of using a pedometer.
2. Put students in small groups and assign each group a different starting pumpkin.
3. Tell the students to set their pedometers to zero.
4. Instruct students to walk or run to the next consecutively numbered pumpkin, which they have to find.
5. Instruct them to record the number of steps on the pedometer and the letter for the secret message onto their record sheet, using the pencils in the pumpkins.
6. Make sure students leave the pencils in the pumpkins for the next person to use.
7. Instruct older students to reset their pedometers each time. Simply have younger students record their running totals.
8. Continue this procedure until the students have traveled to all of the pumpkins and recorded all of the letters.
9. Have students unscramble the letters to decipher the message.
10. Have the older students add their steps to practice math skills.

Safety Considerations

Don't allow students to run around the pumpkin patch with pencils in their hands or pockets.

Adaptation Suggestions

Use fewer pumpkins, make the activity area smaller, or use an easier message.

MONSTER-SIZE SOCCER GHOULS

Quick Description

A very large soccer game with half of the class playing the goalie (defensive) positions and half playing the forward (offensive) positions

Appropriate Ages

5 to 12

Students try to score in every soccer ghoul.

Activity Goals

To practice and improve the skills of dribbling a soccer ball and kicking it into a goal that is guarded by a goalie

Space Required

Gymnasium or field

Key Skills

Dribbling and kicking a soccer ball

Equipment and Preparation

1. Set up enough soccer goals or cones to make goals for half the students in the class.
2. Gather foam soccer balls for half of the students.
3. Attach a Halloween picture on the in each goal.
4. Obtain a timer.

5. Gather four containers and 100 or more objects like poker chips or craft sticks. Two containers contain the chips or sticks, and two are empty.

Activity Procedure

1. Divide the class evenly into two teams: a team of goalies and a team of forwards.
2. Have the goalies each stand by a goal and give each forward a ball.
3. Set the timer for three minutes; tell the forwards they have that much time to score as many goals as they can.
4. Tell students that the ball must be below the goalie's shoulders to count.
5. Tell the team of forwards that they are not allowed to score in the same goal twice in a row.
6. Have the forwards put a chip or stick in a bucket each time they score a point.
7. Instruct the teams to switch when the timer rings (the goalies become forwards and the forwards become goalies).
8. Have the new teams follow the same procedure; put their points in their team's container.
9. Have the teams switch roles every time the timer rings.
10. Continue with this procedure for as long as desired.

Safety Considerations

Use foam soccer balls inside (soccer balls could be used outside). Stress to students the importance of watching where they are running and kicking the ball below the goalies' shoulders.

Adaptation Suggestions

The size of the goals can be adjusted.

GHOST CATCHERS

Quick Description

Manipulative activity

Appropriate Ages

5 to 9

Activity Goals

To improve skill levels in tossing, striking, throwing, catching, and working with a partner

Space Required

Gymnasium or outdoor area

Key Skills

Tossing, striking, throwing, catching, and working with a partner

Equipment and Preparation

Make a "ghost" for every student in your class, or one ghost for every two children (then they can work in pairs and take turns) by covering a small ball (tennis balls work well) with a piece of material (juggling scarves are a good size) and securing it with a rubber band or string.

Activity Procedure

Students should practice the following skills with both their right and left hands, while holding the ball, not the material.

Individual Activities

Tossing and Catching

- Tossing and catching while gradually increasing the height of the toss
- Tossing, clapping hands, and catching
- Tossing, turning around, and catching
- Tossing underneath right leg and catching; tossing underneath left leg and catching

- Tossing from the right hand to the left hand, and from the left hand to the right hand
- Tossing and catching at different body levels

Striking

- Tossing the ghost upward and striking it from underneath with an open hand
- Tossing the ghost upward and striking it forward with an open hand, as in volleyball
- Tossing the ghost upward and striking it forward with an open hand out to the side, as with a tennis forehand
- Striking the ghost with different body parts

Partner Activities

- Throwing underhand to a partner
- Throwing overhand to a partner
- Tossing and striking the ghost underhand to a partner
- Tossing and striking the ghost overhand to a partner
- Tossing and striking the ghost with forehand to a partner

Students can experiment throwing the ghosts by holding on to the material. (Many games such as Clean House can be played using the ghosts. To play Clean House, divide the class into two groups. Mark off a large rectangular area with a dividing line across the width in the middle. Students throw the ghosts to the other team's side, as soon as they are thrown to their side, trying to clean up their side. Stop the game periodically and count the "ghosts." The side with the least ghosts is the cleanest and receives a point. Continue this procedure as long as you like.)

Safety Considerations

Tell students to spread out so they don't bump into each other or hit someone with the ghost.

Adaptation Considerations

Use softer sponge or yarn balls, especially for younger children. Handkerchiefs or smaller pieces of material can also be used for younger children to ensure that they are able to manipulate the "ghost" well. Stress to students when performing the partner portion of the game that they are not to strike the ghost so hard that their partner is injured or afraid of being injured.

STROBE LIGHT ACTIVITIES

Quick Description

Various activities are performed in a darkened room with strobe lights flashing.

Appropriate Ages

5 to 12

Activity Goals

To move to music in a different environment; to develop creativity

Space Required

A classroom or gym with shades drawn or windows covered

Key Skills

Listening to and interpreting music, moving to music

Equipment and Preparation

1. Obtain one or more strobe lights, mylar sheets, and various pieces of equipment (hula hoops, jump-ropes, juggling scarves, and the like).
2. Darken a room.
3. Find some dance music.

Activity Procedure

1. Divide the class into groups.
2. Have the groups take turns dancing, using the different pieces of equipment while the strobe lights are going and dance music is playing.
3. Spend time at the end of class discussing how the use of strobe lights and music made the students feel.

Safety Considerations

Tell students to be extra careful in the darkened room. Turn the lights on when groups are changing positions for turns.

Adaptation Considerations

This is a great activity for students who are self-conscious about doing rhythmic activities and dances; the lights and shadows on the walls make students lose that self-consciousness.

OVERHEAD PROJECTOR TARGETS (SPIDERS, GHOSTS, BATS, OR OTHER THEMES, SUCH AS OUTER SPACE OR ANIMALS)

Quick Description

Students chase and throw yarn or foam balls at projected targets on the wall of a darkened gym or playroom.

Appropriate Ages

5 to 12

Activity Goals

To improve throwing for accuracy

Space Required

Darkened gym or playroom

Key Skills

Accurate throwing

Equipment and Preparation

This activity takes a little extra preparation, but the students just love it.

1. Make transparencies for Halloween, such as spiders, ghosts, or bats (see page 153).
2. Obtain an overhead projector on a rolling cart.
3. Darken a gym or playroom by pulling the shades or covering the windows.
4. Gather six small yarn or foam balls.

Activity Procedure

1. Divide the class into groups of six, more or less, depending on the size of the room.
2. Give each group of six a turn to throw at the targets.
3. Project the targets on the wall and move them around the walls and ceiling.
4. Instruct the throwers to chase the targets and repeatedly throw the balls at them.
5. Have the rest of the class watch from an out-of-the-way area.

Safety Considerations

Stress extra safety while doing this activity in the dark.

Adaptation Suggestions

Use other themes (for example, outer space or animals) for different times of the year. Move the targets slower for students having trouble hitting them with the ball.

NOVEMBER

Thanksgiving

THANKSGIVING SKILLS STATIONS

Quick Description

Throwing skills stations

Appropriate Ages

5 to 12

Activity Goals

To improve form and accuracy while performing underhand and overhand throws

Space Required

Gymnasium

Key Skills

Underhand and overhand throwing

Equipment and Preparation

1. Make a sign for each station and organize the following equipment:

    • Fatten the Turkey—A turkey picture or Thanksgiving paper plate with a turkey picture on it and three beanbags

    • Fill the Horn of Plenty—A picture of a horn of plenty or an upside-down traffic cone and three beanbags

Students aim at the turkey's mouth to practice throwing skills.

- Beat the Indian Drum—A picture of an Indian drum and three beanbags
- Thanksgiving Feast—Pictures of foods from the different food groups and three beanbags
- Thanks—Laminated paper letters to spell the word "Thanks" and three beanbags

2. With masking or floor tape, mark lines on the floor for students to throw from.

Activity Procedure

1. Review the activity procedures for skills stations on pages xii to xiii.
2. Explain each station to the class.
3. Allow each student three attempts per turn to avoid confusion.

Station Descriptions

1. Fatten the Turkey—Students pretend the beanbags are food and throw them at the turkey's mouth.

2. Fill the Horn of Plenty—Students pretend the beanbags are food and throw them at the opening of the Horn of Plenty.

3. Beat the Indian Drum—Students hit (beat) the head of the drum with the beanbags.

4. Thanksgiving Feast—Students must call out which picture of the different food groups they are trying to hit before throwing the beanbags.

5. Thanks—Students must hit the letters in the correct spelling order. Students begin with the letter "T." If they hit it, they aim for the "H" with the second beanbag. If they miss the "H," they try again with the third beanbag. On their next turn, they continue where they left off.

Safety Considerations

Make sure that students who are waiting aren't in the target area or too close to the student taking his or her turn.

Adaptation Suggestions

Raise or lower the targets according to the age of the students. Also, shorten or lengthen the distance from the throwing line to the target according to skill level.

TURKEY TRACK

Quick Description

Ongoing incentive for walking, using pedometers, or walking or jogging laps.

Appropriate Ages

5 to 12

Activity Goals

To improve physical fitness, especially cardiovascular fitness

Space Required

Outdoor or indoor jogging area

Key Skills

Walking or jogging

Equipment and Preparation

1. Weeks ahead of Thanksgiving, decorate a bulletin board with the following:
   - Hang a large turkey in the middle of the bulletin board.
   - Create a border of small turkeys.
   - Put a student's name on each small turkey, using different colors of paper for each class or grade.
2. Gather a large number of craft sticks to count laps or pedometers to count steps.

Activity Procedure

1. Have students count the number of laps or pedometer steps around the track and record them on their turkeys.
2. Have students record extra laps or steps at recess time. Craft sticks can be used to count the laps by handing them to the student after a lap is completed. Using craft sticks, where the students can visually see how many laps they've run, motivates them to continue running as long as they can. Teachers in your school can participate in this also.

Safety Considerations

Ensure that students warm up properly before jogging or walking, especially at recess time.

Adaptation Suggestions

Students can run and walk at their own pace.

TRICKY TURKEY TAG

Quick Description

A chasing and fleeing game that can be played on scooterboards or while running

The students acting as turkeys come out of hiding and try to tag the others.

Appropriate Ages

5 to 12

Activity Goals

To demonstrate bodily control and knowledge of game and safety rules in a game situation

Space Required

Gymnasium

Key Skills

Running, chasing, fleeing, and dodging; maneuvering on scooter-boards

Equipment and Preparation

1. Stand eight or more mats on their sides all over the playing area.
2. Tape a picture of a turkey on each mat.
3. Place a cone for each line of students at one end of the gym.
4. Spread a large number of beanbags or other items like poker chips or craft sticks on the floor at the other end of the gym.
5. Obtain scooterboards, one for each row of students and one for each turkey that will be "it."
6. Differentiate turkeys with a jersey or bandanna to wear.

Activity Procedure

1. Divide students as evenly as possible behind the cones with two to four students in each line.
2. Choose one line of students to be the turkeys first.
3. If scooterboards are used, place one in front of each line and give one to each turkey.
4. Tell the turkeys to hide behind the mats.
5. Explain to the students that the turkeys are hiding behind the mats and guarding their food.
6. On the signal, the students will run or safely ride the scooter-boards to the turkey food and bring a piece back to the line.
7. Have the turkeys try to tag the students.
8. Explain that if students get tagged on the way to the food, they must go back to their lines; if they are tagged with food in their hands, they must return it first and then go back to their lines. Students are not "safe" in the food area.
9. Students in each line continue this procedure until turkeys change.
10. Choose new turkeys frequently.

Safety Considerations

Tell students to use extra caution because many students are moving in different directions. Tell them not to run into the mats because they will fall over. If using scooterboards, sitting, lying down, and kneeling are allowed—no standing or running with just hands on the scooterboard. When students get tagged, tell them to ride the scooterboard back to the line to avoid hitting someone who is sitting down.

Adaptation Suggestions

If some students keep getting tagged and very seldom bring a piece back, let all of the students bring back two pieces and put one back if they get tagged.

TURKEY-TAIL TAG

Quick Description

A chasing and fleeing game

Appropriate Ages

5 to 9

Students pull tails one at a time without touching each other.

Activity Goals

To demonstrate bodily control and knowledge of game and safety rules in a game situation

Space Required

Gymnasium or outdoor area with marked boundaries

Key Skills

Running, chasing, fleeing, and dodging

Equipment and Preparation

Obtain brightly colored juggling scarves or other brightly colored material to use as a "tail."

Activity Procedure

1. Give each student one "tail" (two if you have enough).
2. Show them how to tuck one end of the scarf into the waistband of their pants, back pocket, belt loop, or neckline.
3. Explain that the object of the game is to gather as many tails as possible while keeping your own tail(s); every player is both a chaser and is being chased.
4. Tell the students that they may not touch each other when pulling out a tail and they may not play while carrying the tails in their hands.
5. Designate a safe tail-tucking zone and have the students add pulled tails to their waistbands in the safe zone.
6. Have students continue to play after their tails have been pulled out.
7. Count tails at the end.

Safety Considerations

Emphasize that students must pull tails gently and must not grab another player's clothing or body. Stress that they watch where they are running to avoid collisions.

Adaptation Suggestions

Adjust the size of the playing area to the ability of the students.

THANKFUL TURKEY TAG

Quick Description

A chasing and fleeing game

Appropriate Ages

5 to 12

Activity Goals

To demonstrate bodily control and knowledge of game and safety rules in a game situation; to identify positive aspects of students' lives

After being tagged, a student thinks of something he is thankful for and writes it on the paper.

Space Required

Gymnasium or outdoor area with marked boundaries

Key Skills

Running, chasing, fleeing, dodging, and tagging safely

Equipment and Preparation

1. Write each class's name on a large sheet of paper and attach the paper to the wall of the gym.
2. Place crayons or markers by each sheet of paper.
3. Copy and laminate three or four paper feathers (see page 154), one for each child who is "it," or use real feathers.
4. Use traffic cones to mark boundaries, if necessary.

Activity Procedure

1. Talk to the students about all of the things they have in their lives for which to be thankful.
2. Choose three or four students to be turkeys and give them each a feather.
3. Explain that the turkeys chase the other students and try to tag them with the feathers.
4. Show the students the boundaries for the game. Players who go outside the boundaries are considered tagged.
5. Have students write their names and something they are thankful for on their class's sheet of paper when they are tagged.
6. Tell students to rejoin the game after they have written their item on their class's paper.
7. Change taggers frequently.
8. Begin the game each time by saying "Gobble, gobble."

Safety Considerations

Emphasize the correct way to tag someone with the feather. Students should tag on the arms, legs, back, or chest, not the head or face. They should not push or grab someone when they are trying to tag him or her.

Adaptation Suggestions

Choose more or fewer taggers, depending on the size of the class. Younger students may need help writing their thankful ideas on the paper.

TURKEY IN THE STRAW

Quick Description

Folk dance

Appropriate Ages

5 to 12

Activity Goals

To perform the dance, "Turkey in the Straw," correctly; to improve the ability to work in a group

Space Required

Gymnasium

Key Skills

Walking or sliding, skipping to music in a circle, and working with a partner

Equipment and Preparation

You will need a CD or cassette player and a copy of "Turkey in the Straw."

Activity Procedure

1. Have students become familiar with the music by playing "freeze." Students can skip anywhere in the gym when the music plays, without bumping into anyone, and must "freeze" without falling down, when the music stops.
2. Have younger students flap their arms and quietly say "gobble, gobble" when they freeze.

3. Pair off boys and girls, or allow younger students to choose their own partners. (Younger students usually don't care who their partner is as long as they are dancing. Allowing them to choose their own partners can result in girls with girls and boys with boys).

4. Arrange the couples in a single circle with the girl to the right of the boy; everyone faces the center of the circle.

5. Have everyone join hands.

Measures

1-2: Beginning with the left foot, students take seven walking steps or slides to the left and hold to the count of eight (prepare to change direction).

3-4: Beginning with the right foot, students take seven walking steps or slides to the right and hold to the count of eight.

5: Beginning with the left foot, students walk two steps to the center of the circle (weight should be on both feet) and clap three times.

6: Beginning with the right foot, students walk two steps backwards to the start (weight should be on both feet) and clap three times.

7-8: Partners hook their right elbows and turn in place either walking or skipping.

The dance continues by repeating measures 1 through 8. To make the dance a mixer (changing partners)—and more challenging for the older students— have the boys leave their partners during measure 8 and walk or skip in a counterclockwise direction to meet new partners. Have the girls step in place during this measure. Then the dance continues by repeating measures 1-8.

Safety Considerations

Younger students get very excited when lively music is playing. Emphasize that falling down purposely and playing "crack the whip" when turning is unacceptable behavior.

Adaptation Suggestions

Younger students can use walking steps before they slide or skip. Older students should be able to perform the dance as a mixer.

FAMILY WESTERN NIGHT—CHILI SUPPER—HOCKEY-STICK HORSES

Quick Description

A family event with a Western theme including activities such as line dancing, cowboy roping, circle or square dancing, and playing games

Appropriate Ages

All students and their families

Activity Goals

To promote family health, fitness, and fun

Space Required

Gymnasium, cafeteria, and a few classrooms

Key Skills

Moving to music, listening, and galloping

Equipment and Preparation

1. Have kindergarten students make hockey-stick horses and learn an easy exercise routine or dance with their horses in the weeks preceding the event. (To make the horse, cover the blades of hockey sticks with brown paper, stuffed with newspapers, so that the paper can be decorated with eyes, ears, and so on.)
2. Decorate the school with a Western theme.
3. Arrange for someone to teach easy line dances and circle or square dances that everyone can follow.
4. Send an invitation home to parents about the event.
5. Arrange with your school for the chili dinner.

Activity Procedure

1. Have students and parents eat the chili dinner first.
2. Then, have the kindergarten students perform their Western horse routine.
3. After the entertainment, invite everyone to participate in the various activities.

Safety Considerations

Make sure there is enough room for everyone participating. Don't let participants eat while participating in the activities.

Adaptation Suggestions

The activities are for everyone to participate in and have fun with, whatever their skill level.

CHAPTER 4

DECEMBER
AND JANUARY

Winter, Christmas, Hanukkah, Kwanzaa, and Chinese New Year

WINTER AND HOLIDAY SKILLS STATIONS

Quick Description

Ball-handling and striking stations

Appropriate Ages

5 to 12

Activity Goals

To improve form and accuracy while performing the following skills: rolling, underhand and overhand throwing, overhead volleying, and striking

Space Required

Gymnasium

Key Skills

Rolling, underhand throwing, overhand throwing, striking with a racket and a hockey stick, and overhead volleying

Students practice throwing skills at the Snowball
Fight station.

Equipment and Preparation

Make a sign for each station and organize the following equipment:

1. Trim the Tree—A large green traffic cone or a cone covered with green paper and three hoops or rings

2. Jingle the Bells—A bar with a string of jingle bells suspended from it; three beanbags

3. Light the Hanukkah Menorah—Eight laminated paper candles numbered one through eight; three beanbags

4. Snowball Fight—Three bowling pins and three fleece or sponge balls or rolled-up white socks

5. Put the Head on the Snowman—Two large white circles to resemble a snowman's body; a volleyball

6. Fill the Stocking—A trash barrel with a picture of a Christmas stocking on it, a paddle or racket, and three balls

7. Ice Hockey—Two traffic cones or an indoor goal, one hockey stick, and three hockey pucks

8. Light the Kwanzaa Kinaras—Kwanzaa Kinaras, numbered pictures, and three beanbags

Activity Procedure

1. Review the activity procedures for skills stations on pages xii to xiii.

2. Explain each station to the class.

3. Allow each student three attempts at each station to avoid confusion.

Station Descriptions

1. Trim the Tree—Students throw hoops or rings at the tree, trying to ring the cone.

2. Jingle the Bells—Students try to jingle the bells by throwing beanbags or balls at them.

3. Light the Hanukkah Menorah—Students try to hit the flames or the candles in numerical order.

4. Snowball Fight—Students try to hit the bowling pins with the balls or socks.

5. Put the Head on the Snowman—Students try to hit the spot where the snowman's head should be, using an overhead volley.

6. Fill the Stocking—Students try to hit the balls into the trash barrel using the paddle or racket.

7. Ice Hockey—Students try to hit the hockey pucks into the goal with the hockey stick.

8. Light the Kwanzaa Kinaras—Students try to hit the Kinaras in order.

Safety Considerations

Make sure that students who are waiting their turns are not too close to the student taking a turn, especially at the hockey station. The student who just finished his or her turn can retrieve the balls, beanbags, or hockey pucks for the next student. Otherwise, students should not be moving around.

Adaptation Suggestions

Adjust the distance to the target according to skill level.

REINDEER TRAINING

Quick Description

Cooperative activity in which students push and pull each other on scooterboards

Appropriate Ages

5 to 12

Teaching students the importance of cooperation allows them to pull each other safely on the scooterboards.

Activity Goals

To perform the scooterboard activities cooperatively and safely with a partner

Space Required

Gymnasium

Key Skills

Maneuvering and moving a scooterboard with a partner sitting on it; cooperation

Equipment And Preparation

Eight or more scooterboards and jump-ropes, depending on the size of the class

Activity Procedure

1. Divide the class as evenly as possible into eight lines.
2. Pushing:
   a. The first student sits on the scooter with legs crossed.
   b. The next student in line pushes the first student to a designated turn-around line, and then back to the starting point.
   c. The student sitting on the scooterboard goes to the end of the line.
   d. The student who was pushing takes a turn on the scooterboard.
   e. The next student in line pushes.
3. Continue this procedure as long as you like.
4. Pulling:
   a. The first student sits on the scooterboard with legs crossed, holding a jump-rope folded in half.
   b. The next student in line holds the other end of the rope and pulls the first student to a designated turn-around line, and then back to the starting point.
   c. The student sitting on the scooterboard goes to the end of the line.
   d. The puller sits on the scooterboard, and the next student in line becomes the puller.
5. Continue this procedure as long as you like.

Safety Considerations

Stress the importance of pushing or pulling slowly and in a straight line. Do not allow students to use the whole length of the jump-rope, or "crack the whip," when pulling.

Adaptation Suggestions

Use larger scooterboards with older students. Use round scooterboards to make the activity more challenging.

HANUKKAH DREIDEL GAME

Quick Description

A quiet, small group game

Appropriate Ages

5 to 12

Activity Goals

To learn the story of Hanukkah and how to play the dreidel game

Space Required

Gymnasium, classroom, or outdoor area

Key Skills

Working cooperatively in a small group and following game rules

Equipment and Preparation

1. Read about and discuss Hanukkah (see page 155) and the dreidel with your students to promote understanding of and respect for the Jewish tradition.
2. Collect one empty 2-liter soft drink bottle for every five students in your class.
3. Make a set of four game cards for each group of students by copying and laminating the game cards in this book (see page 156), or make them out of index cards. Each set of game cards should include the following:
   • Nun (N)—The player gets nothing.

- Gimel (G)—The player takes all.
- Heh (H)—The player takes half.
- Shin (S)—The player puts one in.

4. Gather 10 or more small game pieces such as beans, pennies, or pea gravel, for each student.

Activity Procedure

An old custom connected with Hanukkah is a game called dreidel. A dreidel is a four-sided top with a Hebrew letter engraved on each of the four sides. The letters are Nun (N), Gimel (G), Heh (H), and Shin (S). These letters stand for the Hebrew words *nes gadol hayah sham,* which means "a great miracle took place here." They also stand for the Yiddish-German words *nem* (take), *gib* (give), *halb* (half), and *shtel tzu* (add).

To play dreidel, follow these procedures:

1. Divide the class into groups of five (four in a circle and the spinner in the center). Distribute any extra students among the groups.
2. Have each group sit on the floor in a circle with one student in the center.
3. Give each student in the circle one game card to place on the floor in front of him or her, and 10 game pieces.
4. Give the student in the center—the spinner—a 2-liter soft drink bottle.

The game is played as follows:

1. Each player puts one game piece in the center.
2. The spinner spins the bottle.
3. When the bottle stops, the student it is pointing to reads the game card, and the spinner follows those directions:
   a. The spinner will take all of the pieces in the center (Gimel).
   b. The spinner will take half of the pieces in the center (Heh).
   c. The spinner will take none of the pieces in the center (Nun).
   d. The spinner will put one game piece in (Shin).
4. The spinner changes places with a new person who becomes the spinner.

5. When time is up, count the game pieces; the student with the most is the winner.

Safety Considerations

Tell students to be careful not to slip on the game pieces or bottles.

Adaptation Suggestions

Younger students might need older students to help each group.

UNDER-THE-TREE MEMORY GAME

Quick Description

Students look for hidden items underneath a large number of cones.

Appropriate Ages

5 to 12

Activity Goals

To be attentive and honest, and to develop memory in a game situation

Space Required

Full gymnasium

Key Skills

Running, paying attention, and remembering

Equipment and Preparation

You will need about 20 pieces each of 8 different objects or laminated pictures. Spread out a large number of cones on one half of the gym. Randomly hide all of the objects or pictures under the cones.

Activity Procedure

1. Divide the class as evenly as possible into about eight lines at the other end of the gym, facing the cones.
2. Give each line one of the objects or pictures they will be looking for.

This memory game teaches students the importance of paying attention so that they can remember where the hidden items are located.

3. Give the signal for the first student in each row to run to the cones, choose one cone to look under, and lift it up. If the student finds a match to his or her object or picture under the cone, the student takes it back to the line.

4. The next student then goes.

5. Instruct the students that they may look under one cone per turn and take only one piece each time.

6. Tell students waiting their turns to watch when the cones are lifted to see where their pieces are. They should remember those cones when their turns come up.

7. Tell students that if they don't find their pieces when they lift a cone, they must return to the line.

8. Continue this procedure until one line has found all of their pieces.

Safety Considerations

Tell students to be careful not to slip on the pieces on the floor.

Adaptation Suggestions

Younger students can lift more than one cone if their pieces aren't under the first one.

KWANZAA KINARA GAME

Quick Description

Students run and retrieve pieces of the kinaras and arrange them in the correct order for the days of Kwanzaa. This can also be a quiet game.

Appropriate Ages

5 to 12

Activity Goals

To learn about Kwanzaa by playing a game with the kinaras

Space Required

Half or full gymnasium

Key Skills

Running or other locomotor skills, memory, and cooperation

Equipment and Preparation

1. Teach students about Kwanzaa before they play the game (see page 157).
2. Copy, laminate, and cut out the number of sets of the kinaras (see page 158) you will need for your class.
3. Gather enough traffic cones so that there is one cone for each line.

Activity Procedure

1. Divide the class as equally as possible into lines with two or three students in each line.

2. Place a set of the shuffled kinara cards at the other end of the gym opposite each line.

3. Signal the first student in each row to run and retrieve one kinara card and return to the line.

4. Signal the next student to do the same.

5. Continue this procedure until all of the cards have been retrieved.

6. Have the students waiting their turns arrange the cards in order from day one to day seven.

Safety Considerations

Tell students to be careful not to slip on the kinara cards.

Adaptation Suggestions

The running distance can be adjusted according to ability, and a picture of the correct order of the kinaras can be used for matching.

KWANZAA PRINCIPLES MATCHING GAME (NGUZO SABA)

Quick Description

Students match the seven principles of Kwanzaa to the correct African word. This can be an active or a quiet game.

Appropriate Ages

8 to 12

Activity Goals

To learn the principles of Kwanzaa and play a game to remember them

Space Required

Half or full gymnasium

Key Skills

Locomotor skills, memory, and cooperation

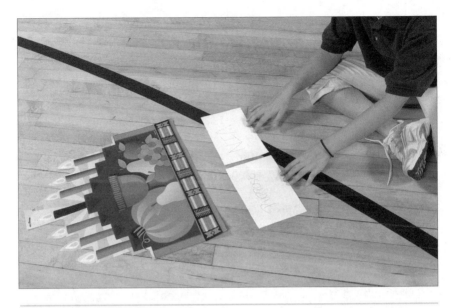

By matching one of the principles of Kwanzaa to the correct African word, students strengthen their memory skills and learn more about African cultures.

Equipment and Preparation

1. Teach students about Kwanzaa before they play the game (see page 157).
2. Copy and laminate the number of sets of the principles of Kwanzaa (see page 159) that you will need for your class.
3. Obtain a cone for each group.

Activity Procedure

1. Divide the class as equally as possible into lines with two or three students in each line.
2. Place all 14 cards that have been shuffled at the other end of the gym opposite each line.
3. Signal the first student to run and retrieve one card and return to the line.
4. Signal the next student to do the same.
5. Students waiting their turns can start matching the principles with their definitions.
6. Continue this until all the cards have been retrieved.

Safety Considerations

Tell students to be careful not to slip on the cards and to watch where they are running, especially where students are on the floor picking up and arranging cards.

Adaptation Suggestions

The running distance can be adjusted according to ability, and a paper with the principles and definitions can be used if students don't remember them.

CATCH THE GINGERBREAD BOY

Quick Description

A chasing and fleeing game

Appropriate Ages

5 to 12

Activity Goals

To demonstrate bodily control and knowledge of game and safety rules in a game situation

Space Required

Gymnasium or outdoor area with marked boundaries

Key Skills

Running, dodging, and tagging safely

Equipment and Preparation

1. Read *The Gingerbread Boy* to the class before they play the game.
2. Make laminated pictures of the characters that chase the Gingerbread Boy, if you want, but the game can be played without them.

Activity Procedure

1. Choose students to be the following characters from *The Gingerbread Boy:* a man, a woman, a bird, a cat, a dog, two or more

children, and a fox. Each student character can hold his or her appropriate picture.

2. Arrange the student characters on a line in the center of the playing area.

3. Arrange the remaining students, all Gingerbread Boys and Girls, on a line at one end of the playing area.

4. Begin with the Gingerbread Boys and Girls saying, "Run, run, as fast as you can! You can't catch me—I'm the Gingerbread Man."

5. Instruct the students that, after the signal (number 4), the characters try to tag the Gingerbread Boys and Girls as they run to the opposite side of the playing area.

6. Tell the students that if the Gingerbread Boys and Girls get tagged, they become helpers in the center and try to catch someone.

7. Instruct the students that the Gingerbread Boys and Girls must say the phrase each time before they run to the opposite side.

8. Choose new characters to be "it" once everyone has been caught.

Safety Considerations

Emphasize that students tag lightly and do not push or grab clothing when tagging someone. Stress that they watch where they are running to avoid collisions.

Adaptation Suggestions

The size of the playing area can be adjusted for ability and class size. If the class is small, use fewer characters to begin the game.

PAPER PLATE SKATING

Quick Description

Manipulative, rhythmic locomotor activity using paper plates.

Appropriate Ages

5 to 12

Activity Goals

To move (skate) to music with a paper plate under each foot, through obstacles, or in a game situation

Students must slide carefully to keep their plate skates on.

Space Required

Gymnasium

Key Skills

Manipulating paper plates with feet to move forward, backward, and sideways and to turn around; performing these skills to music, through obstacles, and in a game situation

Equipment and Preparation

1. Gather two paper plates for each student.
2. Obtain music, such as "The Skaters' Waltz," or "Waltz of the Flowers" from *The Nutcracker Suite*.
3. Gather a large number (five for each line) of traffic cones to use as obstacles to skate through.

Activity Procedure

Demonstrate how students should move (slide) to avoid losing their skates. Have the students perform the following activities using two paper plates as skates:

1. Skate forward, backward, sideways right, sideways left, turn to the right, and turn to the left.
2. Perform the skills in item 1 to music.
3. Create a skating routine to music.
4. Arrange obstacles for students to skate through.
5. Allow older students to have skating races.
6. Play simple games such as tag while skating.

Safety Considerations

Emphasize that students try to stay on their feet and not fall down purposely when skating. Stress that they avoid collisions by watching out for other students when they are skating, especially when they are spinning around.

Adaptation Suggestions

Older students will prefer races and games while wearing the skates.

CHINESE ANIMAL ZODIAC GAME

Quick Description

Students move like the animals in the Chinese Animal Zodiac.

Appropriate Ages

5 to 7

Activity Goals

To develop movement skills and creativity

Space Required

Full or half gymnasium

Key Skills

Various locomotor skills

Students imitate tigers, monkeys, and roosters as they learn the animals of the Chinese Animal Zodiac.

Equipment and Preparation

1. Copy and enlarge the picture of the Chinese Animal Zodiac (see page 160).
2. Read the information about the Chinese Animal Zodiac (see page 161).

Activity Procedure

1. Tell the students about the Chinese Animal Zodiac and show them the picture of it.
2. Scatter students in the playing area.
3. Have one student choose one of the animals to start the game.
4. Signal students to pretend to be that animal until you say, "stop," or blow a whistle.
5. Choose another student to pick the next animal.
6. Continue this procedure until students have pretended to be all of the animals you wanted them to be.

Safety Considerations

Tell students to watch where they are moving and not to touch anyone during the activity.

Adaptation Suggestions

Students can move according to their abilities.

CHINESE DRAGON RUN

Quick Description

Student-led running activity

Appropriate Ages

5 to 12

Activity Goals

To lead a small group in an aerobic activity

The dragon leader holds the dragon face and performs a locomotor movement for the rest to follow.

Space Required

Gymnasium or outside area

Key Skills

Running and other locomotor skills; leading a group

Equipment and Preparation

1. Read the information on Chinese New Year (see page 162).
2. Copy and laminate four or more dragon faces (see page 163), depending on the size of your class.
3. Obtain and play Chinese music, if you like.

Activity Procedure

1. Divide the class as equally as possible into four or five lines with four or five students in each line.
2. Give the leader in each line a dragon face.
3. Signal the dragon leader to lead the line anywhere in the gym or designated area by jogging or performing other locomotor movements.
4. Instruct the students that each line follows the movements of its leader. All lines will be moving at the same time.
5. Tell the students that when you say, "New dragon leader," the leader hands the dragon face to the next student in line and goes to the end of the line.
6. Continue this procedure until everyone has had a chance to be the dragon leader.

Safety Considerations

Stress to students to watch where they are moving so they don't bump into the other lines.

Adaptation Suggestions

The students can perform movements according to their abilities.

FORTUNE COOKIE EXERCISES

Quick Description

Exercise and direction-following game

Appropriate Ages

5 to 12

Activity Goals

To perform exercises and other activities correctly

Space Required

Full or half gymnasium

Key Skills

Performing selected exercises and activities

Equipment and Preparation

1. Write down exercises and activities on pieces of paper (e.g., the type of paper you slide out of a fortune cookie). See page 164 for examples.
2. Put them in a container with Chinese decorations on it, or use a clean Chinese take-out box (the white box with the wire handle).

Activity Procedure

1. Tell students about Chinese New Year (see page 162).
2. Ask students if they have ever eaten a fortune cookie.
3. Tell them that this is their lucky day because it is fortune-cookie exercise day.
4. Have a student choose a fortune and read it to the class. They will then perform the exercise.
5. Have separate boxes for flexibility, strength, and aerobic exercises.

Safety Considerations

Emphasize correct form when performing the exercises.

Adaptation Suggestions

Choose exercises and activities for all skill levels.

FEBRUARY

Valentine's Day, Presidents' Day, Groundhog Day, and Black History Month

Quick Description

Healthy heart and throwing stations

Appropriate Ages

5 to 12

Activity Goals

To perform healthy heart activities, improve throwing skills, and learn about famous African American athletes

Space Required

Gymnasium

Key Skills

Basic step aerobics, overhand and underhand throwing, and knowledge of healthy hearts

A student stands on the bank of the Potomac River, throwing a beanbag across so that it lands on the other side.

Equipment and Preparation

For the stations you will need the following:

1. Step Aerobics—Obtain four or five step-aerobic steppers and music

2. Healthy Heart Exercises—Make a sign that says, "Perform three exercises that make your heart strong, without stopping in between them."

3. Cholesterol—Pictures of foods that are high in cholesterol and some that are not, three beanbags, and tape for the throwing line.

4. Blood Pressure—Make a sign that says "normal blood pressure = 120/80" on it and find pictures of things that will raise blood pressure, such as smoking, unhealthy foods, lack of exercise, and stress. You will need three beanbags and tape.

5. Throwing Across the Potomac—Lightweight balls or beanbags, a container, and mats or tape to mark the throwing lines. (Students should be familiar with George Washington throwing the silver dollar across the Potomac River.)

6. African American Athletes—Stories and pictures of famous African American athletes, a container, three beanbags, and tape.

Activity Procedure

Review the activity procedures for skills stations on pages xii to xiii. Explain each station to the class.

Station Descriptions

1. Step Aerobics—Students take their pulses before and after performing the step aerobics.
2. Healthy Heart Exercises—Students perform three aerobic exercises of their choice without stopping.
3. Cholesterol—Students throw beanbags at the foods that are low in cholesterol.
4. Blood Pressure—Students throw beanbags at the things that raise blood pressure.
5. Throwing Across the Potomac—Students throw beanbags or lightweight balls from one mat or line (over the empty space in the middle–the Potomac River) and onto another mat or container, stepping back each time they are successful.
6. African American Athletes—Students throw beanbags into the container; when they are successful, they read about one of the African American athletes.

Safety Considerations

Leave ample space between stations. Tell students not to stand in the throwing areas.

Adaptation Suggestions

The throwing lines can be adjusted according to ability.

BROKEN HEARTS

Quick Description

Cooperative relay race

Appropriate Ages

5 to 12

By cooperating with her group members, a
student is able to put the puzzle back together.

Activity Goals

To perform the locomotor skills correctly, to work cooperatively in a
group, and to demonstrate knowledge of game and safety rules in a
game situation

Space Required

Full or half gymnasium

Key Skills

Various locomotor skills such as running, galloping, skipping, and
animal walking; participating cooperatively in a group; following
game and safety rules

Equipment and Preparation

1. Obtain a different cardboard Valentine picture for every three or four students in your class. The pictures can be purchased at any card shop around Valentine's Day.
2. Number, laminate, and cut the pictures into equal puzzle pieces.
3. Number the pieces of each valentine on one of the sides. All the pieces for puzzle number one will have a 1 on them. Puzzle number two will have a 2 on its pieces. If the picture is on both sides, make sure the numbers are on the same side so the pieces aren't reversed.

Activity Procedure

1. Arrange the class in single-file lines of three or four students at one end of the playing area behind a line.
2. Give each group a number. Tell them that this is the number on the valentine puzzle pieces that they must retrieve.
3. Mix all of the valentine puzzle pieces together and spread them out across the floor at the other end of the gym.
4. Signal the first student in each row to run to the pieces, choose one piece with the group's number on it, return to the starting line, and tag the next player's right hand.
5. Have students waiting for their turns work together and put the puzzles together.
6. Continue this procedure until all of the puzzle pieces have been retrieved and the puzzles are assembled.
7. Have groups look at each other's completed puzzles, exchange pieces, and race again.

Safety Considerations

Tell students to be careful not to slip on the pieces. Also, stress that they tag right hands to avoid collisions.

Adaptation Suggestions

Make the game easier by purchasing two of each valentine picture, one to cut into puzzle pieces and one for students to use as a guide when assembling the puzzles. You can also make puzzles out of valentine pictures the students have drawn.

AEROBIC VALENTINE BUILDING (LARGEST VALENTINE HEART)

Quick Description

Students run to retrieve pieces to make the largest valentine heart.

Appropriate Ages

5 to 12

Activity Goals

To get a good aerobic workout and to work cooperatively with a group

Space Required

Gymnasium

Key Skills

Running and cooperating

Equipment and Preparation

Spread out hundreds of red and white poker chips or craft sticks on the floor at one end of the gym.

Activity Procedure

1. Divide the class as evenly as possible into lines with two or three students in each line.
2. Signal the first student in each line to run to the pieces, bring one back, and place it on the floor.
3. Have the next student retrieve one piece and place it on the floor.
4. Instruct the students to make a heart shape on the floor with the accumulated pieces.
5. Continue this procedure until all of the pieces have been retrieved.
6. Give students a chance to look at all of the hearts the other groups have made.

The valentine heart gets larger, and the students' hearts get stronger as they have been running to retrieve pieces to place in a heart shape.

Safety Considerations

Tell students to be careful not to slip on the pieces.

Adaptation Suggestions

Have the whole class make one giant heart instead of small groups making multiple small hearts. You can shorten or lengthen the running distance according to ability.

GROUNDHOG SHADOW PARTNERS

Quick Description

Students follow their partners' movements.

Appropriate Ages

5 to 12

Activity Goals

To cooperate with a partner to mirror stationary or locomotor movements

Space Required

Half or full gymnasium

Key Skills

Any movement the students choose; cooperation

Students copy the movements of their partners.

Equipment and Preparation

No equipment is needed unless the movements are done to music. Then you can use a variety of types and tempos of music.

Activity Procedure

1. Divide the class in half so each student has a partner. Three students can work together if there is an odd number. This activity can be done with or without music. Students always like music.

2. Tell students to spread out on the floor.

3. Decide which one of them will be the groundhog and which one will be the shadow.

4. Instruct the groundhog to perform a stationary or locomotor movement and instruct the shadow to copy the movement. (You can designate the type of movement.)

5. Signal the students to reverse roles by saying, "Switch!"

6. Continue this procedure and change partners frequently if you like.

Safety Considerations

Stress to students the importance of watching where they are moving so there are no collisions.

Adaptation Suggestions

Pair off students of like ability. Add equipment like hula hoops, juggling scarves, or balls to make the game more interesting or challenging.

HONEST ABE CENTS GAME

Quick Description

Students throw foam dice into a container, add up their numbers, and collect their points in pretend money.

Appropriate Ages

5 to 12

After throwing the dice into the bucket, students add the numbers on the dice and collect their points in pretend money.

Activity Goals

To improve throwing, math, and money-counting skills and to learn about Abraham Lincoln

Space Required

Full or half gymnasium

Key Skills

Underhand and overhand throwing, addition skills, money-counting skills

Equipment and Preparation

1. Obtain six or more sets of four dice, preferably hand-sized hard foam dice and a large tublike container (laundry basket sized) for each set.

2. Set four dice on each poly spot a short distance away from each tub at one end of the gym.

3. At the other end of the gym, arrange the same number of poly spots for the students to sit behind.

4. Place a few small containers of pretend money behind the students. Remember that the points from the dice will add up quickly, so have a large amount of pretend money on hand.

Activity Procedure

1. Divide the class as evenly as possible, and arrange them in single-file rows at one end of the gym.

2. Signal the first student in each row to run to the dice and throw them one at a time into the tub.

3. Instruct the students to add up the dots on the dice that made it into the tub.

4. Have the students return all four dice to the poly spot for the next student, return to their line, and gather their points in pretend money from the small containers.

5. Emphasize that the procedure is what counts in this game, not who has the most money at the end.

6. Continue this procedure for as long as you want.

Safety Considerations

Students can arrange their money on the floor, but have them keep it away from where other students are running so they don't slip on it.

Adaptation Suggestions

Make the throwing distance shorter, use larger tubs, or just add the dots without turning the points into money.

GEORGE WASHINGTON CHERRY TREE THROWING GAME

Quick Description

A throwing game for accuracy

Appropriate Ages

5 to 12

Students throw balls at each others' cherry trees, trying to knock the objects off.

Activity Goals

To improve throwing for distance and to learn about George Washington

Space Required

Gymnasium

Key Skills

Overhand throwing

Equipment and Preparation

1. Obtain 20 or more cones and 20 or more beanbags, preferably red.
2. Set half of the cones with a beanbag on top of each one on both sides of the playing area. These are the cherry trees.
3. Gather a large number of balls (one for each student) to throw at the cones.

Activity Procedure

1. Divide the class in half and tell them which half of the playing area to go to.
2. Tell students that the cones with the beanbags on top are the cherry trees that they are trying to chop down with the balls. Students may have only one ball in their hands at a time.
3. Give successful students a point.
4. Instruct students to put a beanbag back on the cone if they see it on the floor, in order to continue playing the game.
5. Tell students that they can block the balls away from the cones, but they cannot stand in front of or over a cone to cover it completely.

Safety Considerations

Stress to students that they are throwing at the cones and not at other students.

Adaptation Suggestions

Adjust throwing distance to the students' skill levels.

MARCH

St. Patrick's Day

LUCKY LEPRECHAUN SKILLS STATIONS

Quick Description

Locomotor skills and throwing stations

The students act as leaping leprechauns to leap or jump as far as they can.

Appropriate Ages

5 to 12

Activity Goals

To improve throwing, jumping, leaping, and hopping skills

Space Required

Gymnasium

Key Skills

Underhand throwing, overhand throwing, throwing a flying disk, standing long jump, leaping, and hopping

Equipment and Preparation

Make a sign for each station and organize the following equipment:

1. Over the Rainbow—Volleyball net or rope and three yellow or gold flying disks
2. Blarney Stone Jump—Six or more laminated brown paper "Blarney Stones" with distances ranging from 2 to 7 feet (.6 to 2.1 meters) marked on them and taped to the floor
3. In the Pot of Gold—A trash barrel or box and three yellow or gold beanbags
4. Leaping Leprechauns—Six or more laminated paper shamrocks with distances marked on them and taped to the floor
5. Snakes From Ireland—Six or more jump-ropes arranged in rows
6. Shamrock Score—One large laminated shamrock or three smaller ones, numbered 1, 2, and 3, and three beanbags

Activity Procedure

Review the activity procedures for skills stations on pages xii to xiii. Explain each station to the class:

Station Descriptions

1. Over the Rainbow—Students throw flying disks over a volleyball net, scoring a point if the disk doesn't touch the net.
2. Blarney Stone Jump—Students perform standing long jumps next to the Blarney stones, which mark the distances jumped.

3. In the Pot of Gold—Students throw beanbags into the barrel or box, earning one point for each successful throw.
4. Leaping Leprechauns—Students leap or jump as far as they can. The shamrocks mark the distances.
5. Snakes From Ireland—Students hop over the ropes and back without stepping on them or putting down their nonhopping foot.
6. Shamrock Score—Students throw overhand at the numbers on the shamrocks. They add their points together.

Safety Considerations

Tell students not to crowd the student who is taking a turn. You may want to use a mat for the standing long jump if students are falling backward after they jump.

Adaptation Suggestions

Shorten or lengthen the distances to the target depending on skill level.

BLARNEY STONE STEP-AND-STRETCH RELAY

Quick Description

A slower-moving activity in which students step and stretch from one poly spot (Blarney stone) to another

Appropriate Ages

5 to 12

Space Required

Half or full gymnasium

Key Skills

Flexibility, balance, and judgment of distance

Equipment and Preparation

Two poly spots, or Blarney stones, for each row of students

Students step, stretch, and jump from one Blarney stone to another.

Activity Procedure

1. Divide students as evenly as possible into as many lines as possible because this activity goes a little slower than running-type relays.

2. Have the first student in each line stand on one Blarney stone and hold the second one.

3. Instruct students to judge how far they should toss the Blarney stone they are holding so that they can take a large step from the one they are standing on to that one, without touching the floor.

4. Signal the students to toss their Blarney stone and then leap to it. The students are now standing on the second Blarney stone with both feet and facing the first spot.

5. Have the students stretch and pick up the first stone without letting their feet come off the one they are standing on.

6. Continue this procedure until they reach the finish line. They can run on the way back to their line.

7. Allow the game to continue until everyone has had a turn.

Safety Considerations

Tell students to be careful when they are leaping and stretching. Do warm-up stretches before the activity.

Adaptation Suggestions

This activity does not have to be a race. The distance can be adjusted according to ability.

IRISH AEROBICS OR STEP AEROBICS

Quick Description

Student-led aerobic exercise to Irish music

While listening to Irish music, students follow the leader of step aerobics.

Appropriate Ages

5 to 12

Activity Goals

To lead a small group to perform aerobic exercise to music

Space Required

Half or full gymnasium

Key Skills

Moving aerobically to the beat of the music and leading a small group

Equipment and Preparation

1. Teach students a variety of aerobic exercises or step-aerobic steps.
2. Obtain the music "Irish Washerwoman," "McNamara's Band," or other lively Irish music and a CD or cassette player.
3. Gather steps or mats for each student if you are doing step aerobics.

Activity Procedure

1. Divide students into groups that are as equal as possible with about six students in each group.
2. Have each group make a circle.
3. Assign each student a number 1 through 6.
4. Choose a number to lead the exercises first.
5. Have the student with that number stand in the center of the circle.
6. Play part of the music so the students are familiar with it. Then start it over.
7. Have students in the circle perform the exercise that the leader is doing until you call out another number. This student is the new leader.
8. Continue this procedure until everyone has had a turn.

Safety Considerations

Students should have enough space between them when they make their circles so they don't hit each other.

Adaptation Suggestions

You can whisper an exercise to students who can't think of one.

A REEL JIG

Quick Description

Folk dance

Appropriate Ages

5 to 12

Activity Goals

To perform the dance correctly and to improve the ability to work in a group

Students synchronize their skips and shuffles to perform the "Reel Jig."

Space Required

Full or half gymnasium

Key Skills

Sliding, skipping, and hopping to the beat of the music

Equipment and Preparation

You will need a lively Irish song such as "Irish Washerwoman" or "McNamara's Band" and a CD or cassette player.

Activity Procedure

There are three types of Irish folk dances—jigs, hornpipes, and reels. The jigs and hornpipes are characterized by clogging or tapping steps, and the reels are characterized by shuffling or gliding steps. The Reel Jig is a simple dance I created to include some characteristics of each.

1. Familiarize students with the music by having them skip and slide to it before teaching the dance.
2. Arrange the students in a single circle with hands at their sides, or in a double line with the students facing one another. There are no partners when the dance is performed in a circle. When the dance is performed in a line, partners stand across from one another, leaving enough room so that they don't touch while dancing.
3. The dance is performed in 4/4 time.

Measures

1-2: Beginning with the left foot, students take seven sliding steps to the left and hold on the count of 8.

3-4: Beginning with the right foot, students take seven sliding steps to the right and hold on the count of 8.

5: Students hop on the left foot while tapping the right foot in front (right leg is extended), hop again on the left foot while crossing the right foot over and tapping (right knee is bent), hop again on the left foot while tapping the right foot in front (right leg is extended), then jump on both feet. The movement is done quickly in 4 counts: hop–tap, hop–cross–tap, hop–tap, jump.

6: Repeat measure 5 while hopping on the right foot and tapping with the left foot.

7-8: Repeat measures 5 and 6.

9-10: Stepping back on the right foot, students take eight skipping steps backward.

11-12: Beginning with the right foot, students take eight walking and shuffling steps forward.

13-16: Repeat measures 9 through 12.

The dance continues by repeating measures 1 through 16.

Safety Considerations

To avoid collisions, slow the music down in the beginning and make sure all of the students know which direction they should travel.

Adaptation Suggestions

Use a slower piece of music in the beginning. If some children can't skip backward, they can walk or shuffle. If they can't do the hop–tap step, they can hop, hop, hop, jump.

LIONS AND LAMBS

Quick Description

A chasing and fleeing game

Appropriate Grade

5 to 9

Activity Goals

To demonstrate bodily control and knowledge of game and safety rules in a game situation

Space Required

Gymnasium or large outdoor area

Key Skills

Running, chasing, fleeing, dodging, and tagging safely; developing honesty and good sportsmanship

Equipment and Preparation

Mark off a large playing area with two end lines and a center line. Use traffic cones if necessary.

Activity Procedure

1. Divide the class, as evenly as possible, into two groups—the lions and the lambs.
2. Line up students back to back on the center dividing line. Then have them take three steps away from each other.
3. Choose one student to be the caller.
4. Have the caller try to fool both groups about whom he or she will call by shouting either "l-l-l-lions" or "l-l-l-lambs."
5. If the caller says, "Lions," instruct the lions to chase the lambs to their goal line, trying to catch as many as they can.
6. If the caller says, "Lambs," instruct the lambs to chase the lions to their goal line.
7. Tell the students to count the number of lions or lambs they catch.
8. Have both groups return to their original starting positions.
9. Choose a new caller.
10. Begin the game again.

Safety Considerations

1. Make sure that there are at least 6 feet (about 2 meters) between the two groups at the beginning of each game to prevent collisions when the group turns around to chase.
2. Keep the goal line a safe distance from walls or fences so students don't run into them.
3. Play on grass rather than blacktop to avoid cuts and scrapes if students fall.
4. Emphasize that students tag lightly and don't grab clothing when catching someone.

Adaptation Suggestions

The size of the playing area can be adjusted. The game can be played with the two groups facing each other instead of standing back to back.

POTS OF GOLD OVER THE RAINBOW

Quick Description

Students throw small foam or yarn balls over a net or rope into containers

Appropriate Ages

5 to 12

Activity Goals

To throw at a target for accuracy

To land their balls into the pots of gold, students must throw the balls over the strung rope or net.

Space Required

Full or half gymnasium

Key Skills

Overhand or underhand throwing

Equipment and Preparation

1. Set up one or more volleyball nets or ropes at a low level.
2. Place an equal number of containers such as plastic tubs or buckets on each side of the nets.
3. Gather a large number of small foam or yarn balls. The game lasts longer with as many balls as you have.
4. Decorate the nets or ropes like a rainbow if you like.

Activity Procedure

1. Divide the class as equally as possible among the number of nets you are using.
2. Tell students that the net is the rainbow and the containers are the pots for the gold at the end of the rainbow.
3. Have students throw one ball or piece of gold at a time over the net or rope. Balls that land in a container stay there.
4. Count the gold in the pots at the end of each game.

Safety Considerations

Tell students that even a soft yarn or foam ball can hurt someone, so make sure they aim for the containers.

Adaptation Suggestions

The net or rope can be raised or lowered, and the throwing distance to the containers can be adjusted according to ability.

SHAMROCK SHUFFLE

Quick Description

A running and walking endurance activity in which students (and parents and friends, if you are making this a family event) complete as many laps as they can in a specified time and receive awards.

A student receives a paper shamrock after completing a lap.

Appropriate Ages
5 to 12

Activity Goals
To promote family health and fitness

Space Required
Large outdoor area

Key Skills
Running and walking

Equipment and Preparation
1. Gather a large number of craft sticks, a large box, and a large container (the Pot of Gold).
2. Mark off the running and walking area with cones.
3. Obtain Irish music and a cassette or CD player.
4. Have water available.

5. Make certificates.

6. Gather small prizes and put them in the Pot of Gold.

Activity Procedure

1. Specify the time limit for the activity. During a class period, 15 minutes would be good for students and 30 or more minutes for a family event.

2. Select a couple of students to be leprechauns.

3. Instruct participants to run or walk as many laps as they can in the specified time.

4. Have the leprechauns hand them a paper shamrock or a craft stick for each lap completed.

5. Give out certificates and small prizes from the Pot of Gold for participation at the end of the time limit.

Safety Considerations

All participants should be in good health when they participate in this activity. Participants should be aware that the activity includes walking or running and should be done at his or her own pace. Have all participants drink plenty of water before and during the activity.

Adaptation Suggestions

Children and adults participate at their own paces. Make this a fun and not highly competitive activity.

APRIL

Spring and Easter

APRIL AND EASTER SKILLS STATIONS

Quick Description
Throwing stations

Appropriate Ages
5 to 12

Activity Goals
To improve throwing and rolling skills

Space Required
Gymnasium

Key Skills
Overhand and underhand throwing; rolling

Equipment and Preparation
Make a sign for each station and organize the following equipment:

1. April Showers—Tape laminated paper raindrops (with various numbers on them) to the wall and gather three beanbags
2. Eggs in the Basket—A basket and three unbreakable Easter eggs or small balls

Students practice throwing skills by throwing eggs into the baskets.

3. April Loof—Tape laminated letters for April Loof, purposely spelled backward, to the wall; gather three beanbags
4. Carrot Sticks—A basket and three lummi (12 inch wooden rhythm sticks) or other type of sticks
5. Feed the Bunny—A large picture of a bunny and three small balls or beanbags
6. Over the Puddle—Two tumbling mats and three beanbags

Activity Procedure

Review the activity procedures for skills stations on pages xii to xiii. Explain each station to the class.

Station Description

1. April Showers—Students try to hit the paper raindrops and add together the numbers.
2. Eggs in the Basket—Students try to throw the eggs into the basket.
3. April Loof—Students try to hit the letters in the word "fool," spelled correctly.
4. Carrot Sticks—Students try to toss the sticks into the basket.
5. Feed the Bunny—Students try to hit the bunny's mouth with the beanbags; or lower the picture and have them roll balls at the mouth.
6. Over the Puddle—Students stand on one mat and try to make the beanbags land on the other mat.

Safety Considerations

Make sure that students who are waiting their turns are not too close to the student who is taking a turn. The student who just finished a turn can retrieve the equipment for the next student to avoid collisions from having too many students moving around at once.

Adaptation Suggestions

Shorten or lengthen the distances from the throwing lines to the targets according to skill level.

RACE TO THE CARROTS

Quick Description

This is an ongoing incentive for walking and jogging and for using pedometers.

Appropriate Ages

5 to 12

Activity Goals

To improve physical fitness, especially cardiovascular fitness

Space Required

Outdoor or indoor jogging area

Key Skills

Walking or jogging

Equipment and Preparation

1. Weeks ahead of Easter, put up a bulletin board that looks like a straight race track.
2. Make a paper bunny for each class using your school's die cutter (most schools have one) and write the classroom teacher's name on it.
3. Attach each bunny with a staple along the starting line of the track. (If you use a thumbtack, the bunnies sometimes mysteriously move down the track by themselves or with a little help from students when you're not looking!)
4. At the finish line, attach paper carrots.
5. Cut out the letters for "RACE TO THE CARROTS" and some flowers or other spring decorations to add to the bulletin board.
6. Gather pedometers and craft sticks.

Activity Procedure

1. For each class, have students count the number of pedometer steps or laps around a track using either a pedometer or craft sticks.
2. Designate a student to add up the steps or laps of the whole class each time.
3. Move the class' paper bunny toward the finish line—where the carrots are—according to this number.

Safety Considerations

Students should warm up properly before jogging or walking.

Adaptation Suggestions

Students walk or jog at their own paces.

STEALING EGGS

Quick Description

Aerobic activity in which students run from hoop to hoop taking objects from other students' hoops and placing them in their own

Students steal eggs to get an aerobic workout.

Appropriate Ages

5 to 12

Activity Goals

To get an aerobic workout

Space Required

Gymnasium

Key Skills

Running and stopping

Equipment and Preparation

You will need a hoop or other type of container and five plastic eggs or beanbags for each student.

Activity Procedure

1. Tell students to get a hoop and five eggs.
2. Tell the students to put the hoop somewhere on the gym floor and place the eggs inside the hoop.

3. Signal all students to run to a hoop, "steal" one egg, and place it in their own hoops. Then they run to a different hoop and "steal" another egg.

4. Explain to students that they must go to all of the hoops before they can repeat a hoop and they cannot guard their eggs from being stolen.

5. Continue this procedure until you stop the game.

Safety Considerations

Stress to students to watch where they are running because all of them will be running at the same time. Also tell them to be careful not to slip on the hoops and to place, not throw, the eggs into the hoops.

Adaptation Suggestions

The distance between hoops and the length of the game can be adjusted according to the running ability of the students.

EASTER EGGSERCISE HUNT

Quick Description

Exercise game and Easter egg hunt

Appropriate Ages

5 to 12

Activity Goals

To run and perform exercises correctly

Space Required

Outdoor area

Key Skills

Performing selected exercises

Equipment and Preparation

1. Make enough paper Easter eggs from construction paper so that each student can find five.

Students perform the exercise that is found on the hidden egg.

2. On each egg, write the name of an exercise that the students have performed throughout the year. Older students can do this for you. You can write the same exercise on more than one egg.

Activity Procedure

1. Have some older students hide the eggs for your classes or have the previous class hide them.
2. Show the students a sample of the egg used in the hunt.
3. Tell them that you have hidden enough eggs so each of them can find five.
4. Signal the students to start looking for eggs.
5. Instruct students to return to the exercise area when they have found five eggs.
6. When the whole class has returned, have them space themselves out.
7. Say the name of one of the exercises.
8. Have students who have that exercise on one of their eggs come up to the front and lead the class in that exercise.

9. Continue this procedure until everyone has had a chance to lead.

10. When class is over, collect the eggs or have some students hide them for the next class.

Safety Considerations

Emphasize correct form when students are performing the exercises.

Adaptation Suggestions

You can write other activities on the eggs such as locomotor skills, stunts, and movement challenges.

SCRAMBLED EGGS

Quick Description

Cooperative relay race

Appropriate Ages

5 to 12

Activity Goals

To perform the locomotor skills correctly, work cooperatively in a group, and demonstrate knowledge of game and safety rules in a game situation

Space Required

Gymnasium

Key Skills

Various locomotor skills, such as running, galloping, skipping, and animal walks; cooperating in a group; following rules of a game; and demonstrating knowledge of safety rules while playing a game

Equipment and Procedure

1. Cut out four or more large paper Easter eggs of different colors.

2. Laminate the eggs.

3. Cut the eggs into identical puzzle pieces. Older students can do this for you. They can even decorate one side of the egg. The

number of egg puzzles depends on the size of your class. More eggs mean more turns for the students.

4. Put each puzzle in a container.

Activity Procedure

1. Divide the class as evenly as possible into four or more relay teams.
2. Arrange the teams in single-file lines at one end of the gym, behind a starting line.
3. Place a container of puzzle pieces at the other end of the gym, opposite each line.
4. Signal the first student in each line to perform the designated locomotor skill while approaching the container, take one piece from the container, and return to the starting line.
5. Have the next student retrieve a piece.
6. Continue this procedure until all of the puzzle pieces have been retrieved.
7. Instruct students to work on putting the puzzle together as the race is in progress.

Safety Considerations

Tell students to be careful not to slip on the puzzle pieces and not to slide to the finish line.

Adaptation Suggestions

Locomotor skills can be varied according to ability. Make sure one side of the puzzles is decorated or else it will be too difficult to put together.

BUNNY ANIMAL STICKER MOVEMENTS

Quick Description

Students pretend to be the animals depicted on the stickers on paper bunnies

Appropriate Ages

5 to 8

Activity Goals

To improve motor skills and fitness levels and to develop creativity

After racing to get to the bunnies, students move like the picture of the animal on the bunny.

Space Required

Full or half gymnasium

Key Skills

Running, skipping, galloping, jumping, hopping, and animal walking

Equipment and Preparation

1. Cut a large number (20) of different-colored construction paper bunnies using your school's die cutter (most schools have one).
2. Stick one animal sticker on each paper bunny. Use a large variety of animals.
3. Laminate them if you want them to last longer.

Activity Procedure

1. Spread out the paper bunnies on the floor at one end of the gym.
2. Divide the class as evenly as possible into lines with about three students in each line.
3. Tell the students which locomotor skill they must use to get to the paper bunnies.
4. When they get there, have them look at one animal sticker and

move like that animal to get back to their lines. They do not bring the sticker bunny back with them.

5. Have the next student in line begin.

6. Continue this procedure for as long as you like.

7. Have students waiting their turns guess what animals the other students are.

Safety Considerations

Tell the students to keep their "animal" heads up so they don't crash into anyone.

Adaptation Suggestions

The students perform their animal movements at their own skill levels.

EGG BALANCE RELAY

Quick Description

Students balance plastic eggs on spoons while walking on a line on the floor.

Appropriate Ages

5 to 12

Activity Goals

To improve balancing skills

Space Required

Full or half gymnasium

Key Skills

Balance

Equipment and Preparation

1. Gather 100 or more plastic eggs and eight or more spoons and containers.

2. Make a line of tape for each row of students.

3. Spread out the eggs on the floor at one end of the gym. Contain them with mats or put them in a few tubs.

A student practices balancing skills while carefully walking with an egg in her spoon.

Activity Procedure

1. Divide the class as evenly as possible into lines of two to four students.
2. Place a container and a spoon in front of each line.
3. Signal the first student to run to the eggs, choose an egg, place it on the spoon, hold the spoon with egg with one hand, and walk back on the tape line to the starting point.
4. If the egg falls off the spoon, have the student retrieve the egg and continue from where the egg fell off.
5. Explain to students that they may not hold the egg on the spoon in any way and if they don't stay on the line, their egg is put back.
6. Continue this procedure until all of the eggs are gone. Students with the most eggs at the end win.

Safety Considerations

Tell students to avoid stepping on the eggs.

Adaptation Suggestions

You can shorten or lengthen the distance to the eggs. If you have balance beams, students can try walking on the balance beam while balancing the egg on the spoon.

BUNNY BLAST

Quick Description

This activity is a yearly tradition for me. Every spring, I rent a bunny costume and choose students to wear it. All of my classes do Bunny Boogie Exercises, the Hokey Pokey, the Duck Dance, and of course, the Bunny Hop. This is a good family night activity.

Appropriate Ages

5 to 10; older students earn the reward of being the bunny or the bunny's helper

Activity Goals

To perform rhythmic activities, exercises, and dances to music; to allow older students a chance to lead and help the younger ones; to have a lot of fun with friends and family!

Space Required

Half of a large gym—a large circle

Key Skills

Exercises that students know such as the Hokey Pokey, the Duck Dance, the Bunny Hop, and other dances your students like to do

Equipment and Preparation

1. Obtain the music ("Here Comes Peter Cottontail," "Hokey Pokey," "Duck Dance," and "Bunny Hop") and teach the dances throughout the year so students are prepared.
2. Obtain a bunny costume or make a pair of bunny ears out of construction paper.
3. Choose students to wear the costume or constructed ears and to be the helpers.
4. Make some giant paper carrots for the bunny.
5. Have the younger children make and wear bunny ears, as well.

Activity Procedure

1. Before the classes come to the gym, hide the designated bunny somewhere.
2. Seat students in a circle.

The bunny leads the class in a popular dance, such as the Bunny Hop.

3. Play the song "Here Comes Peter Cottontail." I really build it up that when the bunny hears this song he will come out. The younger ones really get excited.
4. Have the bunny make an entrance, walk around, and wave to the students.
5. Do Bunny Boogie exercises while listening to *Bunny Boogie.*
6. Have the bunny lead the exercises.
7. Perform the Hokey Pokey, the Duck Dance, and the Bunny Hop—with the bunny, of course.

Safety Consideration

If you actually rent a costume, have a bunny helper lead the bunny around. Tell students to stay on their feet during the dances.

Adaptation Considerations

If this is a family night, students can teach their family members the dances ahead of time or briefly review them.

MAY, JUNE, AND JULY

Cinco de Mayo and Summer Fun

CHAPTER 8

CINCO DE MAYO PIÑATA JUMPING GAME

Quick Description

Students jump, trying to touch balloons of various heights.

Appropriate Ages

5 to 12

Activity Goals

To improve jumping skills and to learn about Cinco de Mayo

Space Required

Half or full gymnasium

Key Skills

Jumping for height

Equipment and Preparation

1. Obtain a rope and string it across one or more volleyball standards at a high level.
2. Write English and Spanish numbers on the balloons (see page 165).
3. Attach 10 balloons to the rope at different heights. Don't put them too close together.

Students jump and touch the highest balloon (piñata) that they can.

4. Teach students about Cinco de Mayo (see page 166) and the piñata.

Activity Procedure

1. Have students jog around the gym or have them start from a stationary position.
2. Tell students to jump and reach for the lowest balloon.

3. Explain that if they touch it, then on their next jump, they reach for the next-higher balloon. But if they miss, they continue trying to touch that balloon.

Safety Considerations

Tell students to wait until the person ahead of them gets out of the way before jumping.

Adaptation Considerations

The balloons can be adjusted for various skill levels.

CINCO DE MAYO JUMPING BEAN GAME

Quick Description

A jumping and Spanish counting game for endurance

Appropriate Ages

5 to 12

Activity Goals

To improve jumping skills and endurance

Space Required

Half or full gymnasium

Key Skills

Jumping and endurance

Equipment and Preparation

1. Teach the students about Cinco de Mayo (see page 166).
2. Tape 10 lines on the floor, or use jump bands (elastic bands with loops on the ends) between cones.
3. Label the lines in English and Spanish (see page 165).

While counting in Spanish, students try to jump over all 10 lines.

Activity Procedure

Have students jump over as many lines (one at a time) in succession as they can, landing on both feet each time.

Safety Considerations

Tell students to stop jumping if they feel like they are going to fall.

Adaptation Considerations

Students jump according to their abilities.

SOMBRERO UNO–DIEZ (ONE–TEN)

Quick Description

Students run to retrieve paper sombreros and arrange them in order from 1 to 10 in Spanish.

Appropriate Ages

5 to 12

Activity Goals

To improve motor skills and learn the numbers 1 through 10 in Spanish

Space Required

Full or half gymnasium

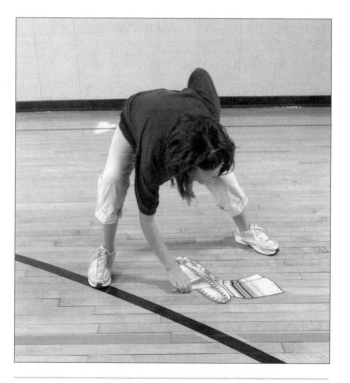

Students arrange the sombreros in numerical order in Spanish.

Key Skills

Running or other locomotor skills

Equipment and Preparation

1. Copy, laminate, and cut apart six sets of the sombreros (see page 167).

2. Make a copy of the Spanish and English number chart (see page 165).

3. You play Mexican music during this activity, so you will need a CD or cassette and a CD or cassette player.

Activity Procedure

1. Divide the class as equally as possible into six or more lines depending on the size of your class.

2. Place a set of shuffled sombreros at the other end of the gym, opposite each line.

3. Signal the first student to run to the sombreros and bring one back, and then go to the end of the line.

4. Have the next student retrieve a sombrero.

5. Continue this procedure until all of the sombreros have been retrieved.

6. Have the students arrange the sombreros in numerical order.

Safety Considerations

Tell students to be careful not to slip on the sombreros.

Adaptation Suggestions

Hang the Spanish-to-English chart for the students to use during the game.

SPACE STATION BUILDING

Quick Description

Students use various motor skills to travel to a variety of equipment used to build space towers. Then throwing skills are used to knock the buildings down.

Appropriate Ages

5 to 12

Activity Goals

To perform motor skills correctly, work cooperatively in a group, develop creativity, and follow safety rules

Space Required

Gymnasium

Key Skills

Using scooterboards, throwing, balancing

Equipment and Preparation

1. Get cones, cardboard tubes, shoeboxes, pieces of Styrofoam—anything that would be good to build a tower—and spread it out at one end of the gym.
2. Designate with a poly spot where each group will build their tower, where each group will sit, and from where they will throw.
3. Gather enough balls and scooterboards to have one for each group.

Activity Procedure

1. Divide the class as evenly as possible and arrange them in single-file rows at one end of the gym.
2. Signal the first student to ride the scooterboard, either sitting, lying down, or kneeling, to the other end of the gym where the building pieces are.
3. Have the student place one piece in position near the poly spot and ride the scooterboard back to his or her group.
4. Have the next student follow the same procedure.
5. Note that as the tower becomes taller, balancing the pieces becomes more difficult. If the tower collapses during the building process, the students can fix it.
6. When all of the pieces are used and the towers are finished, arrange each group on another poly spot that is a shorter distance away (when they throw, they move closer to the towers)

from a tower that they did not build. Be sure to move scooter-boards out of the way.

7. Have each student take one turn throwing a ball at the tower to knock it down. All of the pieces must be knocked over.

8. Once an entire tower has been knocked over, the game ends. Let students throw longer if one is leveled right away.

Safety Considerations

Stress scooterboard safety rules, such as no standing on the scooter-boards, don't push an empty scooterboard at someone, and tie back long hair and clothing so they don't get caught in the wheels.

Adaptation Suggestions

Make the distances for the scooterboard ride and throwing shorter or longer, depending on skill level. Also, various locomotor skills can be used instead of scooterboards.

FILL IT UP

Quick Description

An aerobic water-transferring team race

Students have to walk or run continuously, while being careful not to spill any water.

Appropriate Ages

5 to 12

Activity Goals

To run or walk fast continuously, work cooperatively in a group, and demonstrate knowledge of game and safety rules in a game situation

Space Required

Outdoor area

Key Skills

Running or walking; following game and safety rules

Equipment and Preparation

1. Get two buckets for each team.
2. Get one measuring cup.
3. Gather enough very small plastic or paper cups for each student to have one (the soft plastic cups hold up the best).
4. Find a source of water near the playing area and fill one bucket for each team.

Activity Procedure

1. Explain the race to the class.
2. Divide the class into teams of three to five students.
3. Arrange each team, single file, at one end of the playing field behind a bucket of water.
4. Place an empty bucket at the other end of the playing area, opposite each team.
5. Make sure each team knows which buckets are theirs.
6. Give each student a small cup.
7. Signal all students to fill their cups with water from the bucket in front of them, run to the empty bucket, pour in the water from their cups, run back to the starting bucket, and fill their cups again.
8. Leave enough space between the teams for all students to run at once to achieve an aerobic benefit.
9. Tell students that they may place one hand over the top of the cup to prevent the water from spilling when they run.

10. Continue this procedure until you stop the game.

11. Measure the water in each bucket. The team with the most water wins.

Students get a good aerobic workout because they are so busy transferring the water that they don't realize how long they have been running.

Safety Considerations

To avoid collisions, tell students to watch where they are running and to keep to the right. Also, warn them that the playing area might become slippery when it gets wet.

Adaptation Suggestions

You can adjust the distance between the buckets or the time limit according to ability.

BAREFOOT AND MARBLEOUS

Quick Description

A marble-transferring relay using only the feet

Appropriate Ages

5 to 12

Activity Goals

To manipulate marbles with the feet, work cooperatively in a group, and demonstrate knowledge of game and safety rules in a game situation

Space Required

Full or half gymnasium

Key Skills

Manipulating objects with the feet, and following game and safety rules

A student works on picking up a marble with his toes.

Equipment and Preparation

1. Gather 100 or more marbles, a hula hoop (or a mat), a container (flying disks turned over work great), and masking tape for each group of students.
2. Tape one hoop for each group to the floor at one end of the playing area, opposite where each group will be sitting.
3. Place about 25 marbles in each hoop. The number does not have to be equal.

Activity Procedure

1. Divide the class as evenly as possible into small groups.

2. Have the students remove their shoes and socks and put them away from the playing area.

3. Line students up at one end of the gym behind a container.

4. Make sure each group knows which hoop is theirs.

5. Signal the first student in each group to run to the hoop, pick up only one marble with his or her toes, and run, hop, or perform any other locomotor movement back to the container.

6. Have the student release the marble into the container and go to the end of the line.

7. When the marble is released, have the next student retrieve a marble in the same manner.

8. Continue this procedure until you stop the game.

9. If a marble gets away, have the student retrieve it with his or her feet.

10. At the end of the game, have students count the marbles in their containers.

Safety Considerations

Make sure the gym floor is clean and free of any foreign objects that might injure a student. Also clear away tables and chairs so there is no possibility of students stubbing their toes. Make sure shoes and socks are away from the playing area and that hoops are taped to the floor so students don't slip on them.

Adaptation Suggestions

Adjust the distance from the hoops to the containers according to ability. Have younger students pretend to be animals that use their feet to pick up items.

MUMMY-WRAPPING ROLLING RELAY

Quick Description

A cooperative relay race

Appropriate Ages

5 to 12

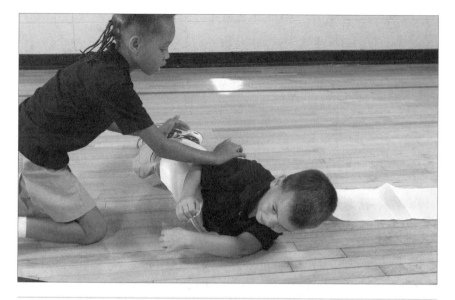

Students must work on their cooperative skills in order to wrap and roll the mummy.

Activity Goals

To work cooperatively as part of a team

Space Required

Grassy area or gymnasium with mats

Key Skills

Cooperation and rolling

Equipment and Preparation

1. Get white butcher-block paper, rolls of paper towels, or gauze. You will need enough to wrap five or six students, depending on the size of your class.
2. Gather enough traffic cones to have one for each team.

Activity Procedure

1. Spread out a sheet of paper or gauze on the ground for each team.

2. Leave plenty of space between the teams.

3. Line up each team behind the paper or gauze.

4. Signal one student to lie down on the paper or gauze.

5. Have his or her teammates wrap and roll the student to the cone.

6. Then have them help the mummy stand up and jump back to the starting line.

7. Continue this procedure until all of the students on the team have been wrapped and rolled. First team finishing correctly wins.

Safety Considerations

Make sure the playing area is free of sticks and rocks. Tell students to be extra careful when rolling and helping the mummy jump. Roll the mummy on mats if you are playing inside.

Adaptation Suggestions

The length of the rolling area can be adjusted according to ability.

FIREWORKS BALLOON TAG

Quick Description

A balloon-popping, chasing, and fleeing game

Appropriate Ages

5 to 12

Activity Goals

To demonstrate bodily control and to follow game and safety rules in a game situation

Space Required

Large outdoor area marked with boundaries, or gymnasium

Key Skills

Running, chasing, fleeing, dodging, and stepping on balloons safely

Students chase each other carefully, trying to step on and pop the others' balloons.

Equipment and Preparation

1. Gather enough balloons for each student to have one.
2. Have older students inflate the balloons and tie a string on each balloon ahead of time for you.

Activity Procedure

1. Have each student tie the balloon on a string around his or her ankle so that the balloon is touching the ground but not tripping the student when he or she runs.
2. Signal the players to chase each other, trying to step on a balloon to pop it.
3. Explain that players must also prevent their own balloon from being popped.
4. Tell the students that they may not hold other players while trying to pop the balloon. Only feet may be used.

5. Tell students that they may continue playing after their balloon has been popped.

Safety Considerations

Make sure that the string isn't too long so students don't trip over it. Keep the boundary lines away from walls or fences to avoid accidents. Stress that students watch where they are running to avoid collisions, because most eyes will be on the balloons.

Adaptation Suggestions

Adjust the size of the playing area according to ability. Inflate extra balloons for the younger students who will be disappointed when their balloons pop.

PLANETS' ORBIT RELAY

Quick Description

A cooperative circle relay race

Appropriate Ages

5 to 12

Activity Goals

To work cooperatively with a group and to learn about the planets

Space Required

Gymnasium

Key Skills

Running, cooperating, and learning about the planets

Equipment and Preparation

Students should have some knowledge about the planets before playing this game.

1. Copy, laminate, and cut apart enough sets of planet cards (see page 168) for every three students in your class. Discuss knowledge about the planets.

2. Get a traffic cone for each group.

3. Get one scooterboard for each group. (This activity can be performed using running or other locomotor skills, or with scooterboards.)

Activity Procedure

1. Divide the class into groups of three and arrange the students on a large circle like the spokes of a wheel.

2. Place a set of shuffled planet cards for each group in the center of the circle, opposite each group.

3. Signal the first student in each group to run counterclockwise around the circle or orbit, tag the next student in line, and retrieve a planet card from his or her group's pile.

4. Continue this procedure until all of the cards have been retrieved.

5. Have students put the planets in order according to their distances from the sun. Groups that arrange the cards correctly win.

Safety Considerations

Tell students to be careful not to lose their balance when running in a circle. Also stress that they watch out for other students when retrieving the cards to avoid collisions.

Adaptation Suggestions

Have the order of the planets available for the students to look at while arranging their cards. Other locomotor skills can be used instead of running.

HIEROGLYPHICS SECRET MESSAGE HUNT

Quick Description

Students run from one picture clue to the next to decipher the secret message

Appropriate Ages

5 to 12

Activity Goals

To get an aerobic workout while following clues and unscrambling letters

Space Required

Outdoors or indoors

Key Skills

Following directions; running or walking

Equipment and Preparation

1. Gather enough index cards, pencils, markers, and masking tape to make 10 to 15 picture cards of things in your activity space, such as a door, tree, window, water fountain, and so on.
2. Write one letter of the secret message on each picture card.
3. Set the course up by taping the next picture card on the previous landmark.
4. Leave a pencil by each picture card so students aren't running around with them.

Activity Procedure

1. Divide class into pairs or small groups.
2. Give each group an index card.
3. Designate which picture card each group starts at so the class is spread out. A few students can start at a door.
4. Have students write down the clue letter on their cards. If there is a tree card taped to the door, students run to the tree, where they get the next card and clue.
5. Continue this procedure for all the cards until all of the clue letters have been collected.
6. Have students unscramble the letters.

Safety Considerations

Leave pencils by the clue cards so students aren't running around with them.

Adaptation Suggestions

Make the distances between clues shorter or longer depending on ability. Students can walk instead of run. Give hints for the message. You can use three different words and write the letters in three different colors to make unscrambling easier.

OLYMPIC OPENING CEREMONY AND EVENTS

Quick Description

A school-wide or family event that recreates an Olympic opening ceremony including international dances

Appropriate Ages

All students and their families and teachers

Activity Goals

To promote family fitness and school-wide fun

Student parade with the Olympic flag and torch during the Olympic festivities.

Space Required

Gymnasium or outdoor area

Key Skills

A variety of easy international dances learned in physical education classes

Equipment and Preparation

Students will prepare an Olympic opening ceremony in physical education classes before the day of the program. This can include the following:

1. The Parade of Nations—Students can make paper flags of different countries. Purchase or make Olympic and American flags. Participants can then parade around the gym.

2. Obtain the National Anthem, Olympic music, and music for the dances you choose to do. Teach students these dances, and students can in turn teach the dances to their parents, if they want to.

3. Make an Olympic torch from a small cone turned upside-down. Fill the cone with orange tissue paper to look like the torch is holding a flame. Also make an Olympic cauldron from a bucket and orange tissue paper. Select 10 students to be the torch bearers and instruct them how to pass the torch and light the cauldron.

4. Purchase five or more helium balloons to symbolize the doves of peace, or make white paper birds on sticks. Choose students to carry them. Incorporate positive behavior such as being safe, cooperative, kind, respectful, peaceful, and responsible.

5. Make a copy of the Olympic Oath. Choose a student to read it. Discuss the meaning of it with the students.

6. Find a long pole for the Limbo dance.

7. Purchase Chinese ribbons on sticks.

Activity Procedure

1. Parade of Nations—Students, parents, and teachers parade around the gym or outdoor area in a large circle with their flags to Olympic music. Everyone then stops and stays in a circle.

2. National Anthem—Play the music and have everyone sing along.

3. Olympic Torch Relay—10 or more students are selected ahead of time to carry and pass the torch to each other while jogging around the gym or outdoor area, while the Olympic music plays in the background.

4. Olympic Flame Lighting—The last torch bearer pretends to light the Olympic cauldron.

5. Olympic Oath—A student is chosen to read the Olympic Oath, and everyone repeats it: In the name of all competitors, I promise that we shall take part in these Olympic Games, respecting and abiding by the rules which govern them, in the true spirit of sportsmanship, for the glory of sport and the honor of our teams.

6. Release of the Doves—Five or more students release white helium balloons or wave white paper birds on sticks in the air.

7. International Dances—Students will demonstrate the dances for the adults. Students can perform partner dances with their parents and teachers. All other dances are performed in a large group. Possible dances include the following:
   - Mexican Hat Dance
   - A Reel Jig
   - The Hora
   - The Polka
   - The Limbo
   - The Hula
   - Chinese Ribbon Dance

Safety Considerations

Make sure there is enough room for everyone to participate safely.

Adaptation Suggestions

Choose activities suitable for everyone, young and old.

APPENDIX

REPRODUCIBLE AWARDS AND MATERIALS

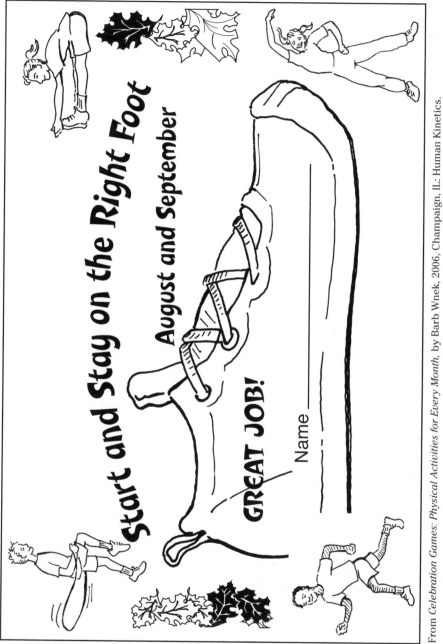

Start and Stay on the **Right Foot**

August and September

GREAT JOB!

Name _____

From *Celebration Games: Physical Activities for Every Month*, by Barb Wnek, 2006, Champaign, IL: Human Kinetics.

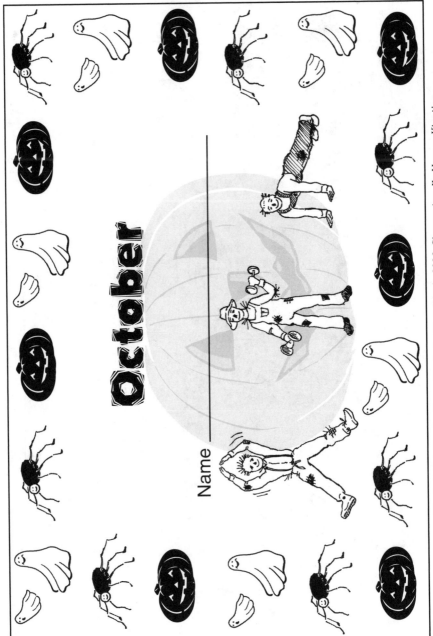

Name

October

From *Celebration Games: Physical Activities for Every Month*, by Barb Wnek, 2006, Champaign, IL: Human Kinetics.

November

Name _____

From *Celebration Games: Physical Activities for Every Month*, by Barb Wnek, 2006, Champaign, IL.: Human Kinetics.

Name _____

February

Name

March

Name _____

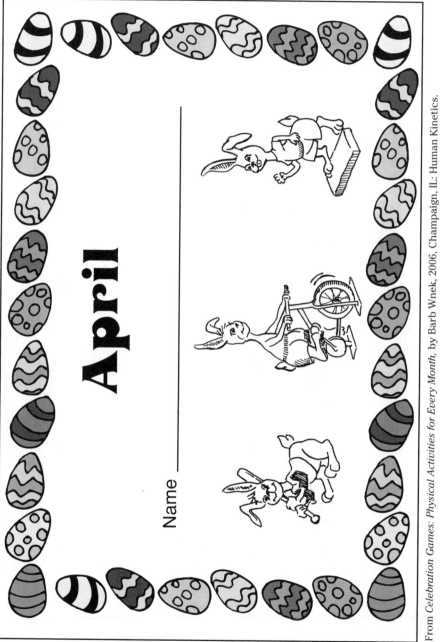

April

Name _____

May, June, and July

Name _____

From *Celebration Games: Physical Activities for Every Month,* by Barb Wnek, 2006, Champaign, IL: Human Kinetics.

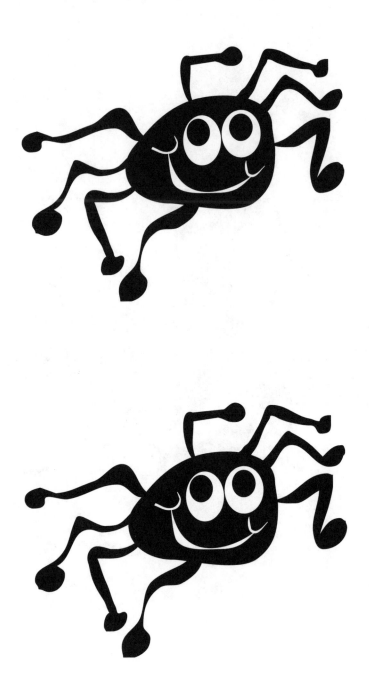

From *Celebration Games: Physical Activities for Every Month,* by Barb Wnek, 2006, Champaign, IL: Human Kinetics.

I Escaped From the Spiders in Physical Education Class

Name

From *Celebration Games: Physical Activities for Every Month*, by Barb Wnek, 2006, Champaign, IL: Human Kinetics.

PEDOMETERS IN THE PUMPKIN PATCH

Write down the number of steps it takes you to get to each pumpkin.
Reset your pedometer each time.

Pumpkin 1 to 2 _____ steps

Pumpkin 2 to 3 _____ steps

Pumpkin 3 to 4 _____ steps

Pumpkin 4 to 5 _____ steps

Pumpkin 5 to 6 _____ steps

Pumpkin 6 to 7 _____ steps

Pumpkin 7 to 8 _____ steps

Pumpkin 8 to 9 _____ steps

Pumpkin 9 to 10 _____ steps

Pumpkin 10 to 11 _____ steps

Pumpkin 11 to 12 _____ steps

Pumpkin 12 to 13 _____ steps

Pumpkin 13 to 14 _____ steps

Pumpkin 14 to 1 _____ steps

From *Celebration Games: Physical Activities for Every Month,* by Barb Wnek, 2006, Champaign, IL: Human Kinetics.

From *Celebration Games: Physical Activities for Every Month,* by Barb Wnek, 2006, Champaign, IL: Human Kinetics.

From *Celebration Games: Physical Activities for Every Month,* by Barb Wnek, 2006, Champaign, IL: Human Kinetics.

HANUKKAH HISTORY

Hanukkah is a Jewish holiday, called the Festival of Lights, which begins on the 25th of Kislev and lasts eight days. It has been celebrated for 22 centuries. It commemorates the victory of the Maccabees (led by Judah) over the Hellenistic Syrians (led by Antiochus) around 165 BCE. The Temple of Jerusalem was reclaimed and rededicated. The Temple's eternal light burned for eight days. This was said to be a miracle because legend says that there was only enough oil left to have the light burn for one day. The eight days of Hanukkah are symbolized by the lighting of eight candles in a holder called a menorah. The middle candle, which makes a total of nine candles, is called the shammes. It is used to light the other eight candles, each representing one night of Hanukkah.

From *Celebration Games: Physical Activities for Every Month,* by Barb Wnek, 2006, Champaign, IL: Human Kinetics.

Nun (N)

The player gets nothing.

Gimel (G)

The player takes all.

Heh (H)

The player takes half.

Shin (S)

The player puts one in.

From *Celebration Games: Physical Activities for Every Month,* by Barb Wnek, 2006, Champaign, IL: Human Kinetics.

KWANZAA CELEBRATION

Kwanzaa is a celebration of African heritage. It was created by Dr. Maulana Karenga in 1966. Today's celebration of Kwanzaa lasts seven days, from December 26th to January 1st. Each of the seven days is dedicated to one of the seven principles know as "Nguzo Saba," and each day a candle is lit to represent that principle. The candelabrum is called a kinara.

Day	*Candle*	*Principle*
Day 1	Middle black candle	Umoja (Unity)
Day 2	Innermost red candle	Kujichagulia (Self-determination)
Day 3	Innermost green candle	Ujima (Collective work and responsibility)
Day 4	Middle red candle	Ujamaa (Cooperative economics)
Day 5	Middle green candle	Nia (Purpose)
Day 6	Outermost red candle	Kuumba (Creativity)
Day 7	Outermost green candle	Imani (Faith)

From *Celebration Games: Physical Activities for Every Month,* by Barb Wnek, 2006, Champaign, IL: Human Kinetics.

From *Celebration Games: Physical Activities for Every Month,* by Barb Wnek, 2006, Champaign, IL: Human Kinetics.

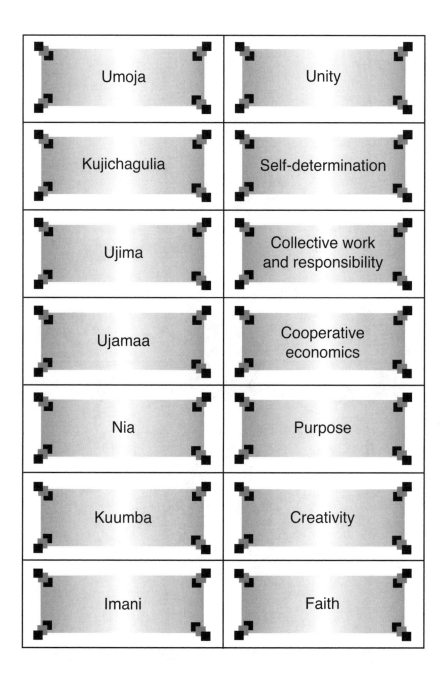

Umoja	Unity
Kujichagulia	Self-determination
Ujima	Collective work and responsibility
Ujamaa	Cooperative economics
Nia	Purpose
Kuumba	Creativity
Imani	Faith

From *Celebration Games: Physical Activities for Every Month,* by Barb Wnek, 2006, Champaign, IL: Human Kinetics.

From *Celebration Games: Physical Activities for Every Month,* by Barb Wnek, 2006, Champaign, IL: Human Kinetics.

CHINESE ANIMAL ZODIAC CALENDAR

The Chinese lunar calendar is based on the cycles of the moon, which differs from the Western solar calendar. The Chinese have used the Western calendar since 1911, but the lunar calendar is still used for some festive occasions. The Chinese animal signs are a 12-year cycle for dating the years. The order is rat, ox, tiger, rabbit, dragon, snake, horse, sheep, monkey, rooster, dog, and boar (pig). For example, the year 2000 was the Year of the Dragon. Chinese folklore states that each animal represents certain characteristics in a person, such as the horse being cheerful and popular.

From *Celebration Games: Physical Activities for Every Month,* by Barb Wnek, 2006, Champaign, IL: Human Kinetics.

CHINESE NEW YEAR

The Chinese greeting for the New Year is "Gung Hay Fat Choy." In China, it is the most important holiday, which is celebrated sometime between January 21st and February 19th. The celebration includes setting off firecrackers to chase away evil spirits and participating in a parade of a large dragon, drums, gongs, and lion dancers. The Chinese celebrate New Year all over the world.

From *Celebration Games: Physical Activities for Every Month,* by Barb Wnek, 2006, Champaign, IL: Human Kinetics.

From *Celebration Games: Physical Activities for Every Month,* by Barb Wnek, 2006, Champaign, IL: Human Kinetics.

You will make your abdominal muscles stronger if you do 20 sit-ups.	Your gluteus maximus muscle will get stronger if you do 20 mountain climbers.
Jog anywhere in the gym until the whistle blows to make your heart strong.	Do straddle stretches to make your hamstring muscles more flexible.
Do 20 arm curls to make your bicep muscles stronger.	Do 10 pushups or modified pushups to make your bicep, tricep, pectoral, and deltoid muscles stronger.
Jump 20 times as high as you can to make your legs strong.	Raise and lower your arms over your head to make your deltoid and bicep muscles stronger.
Skip anywhere in the gym and lift your knees high to make your heart strong.	Do 20 jumping jacks for allover conditioning.

From *Celebration Games: Physical Activities for Every Month,* by Barb Wnek, 2006, Champaign, IL: Human Kinetics.

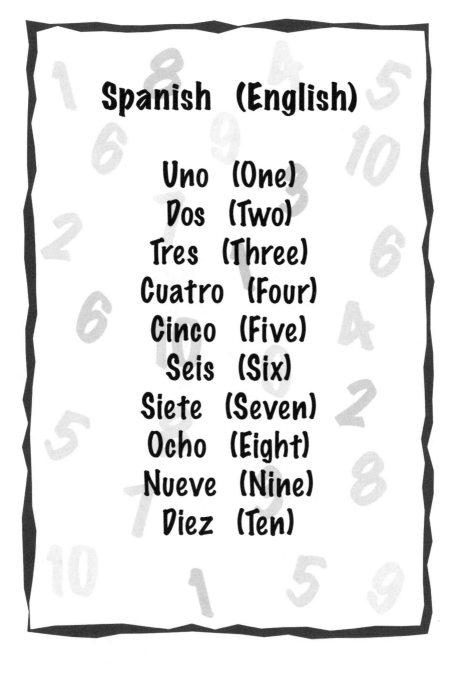

Spanish (English)

Uno (One)
Dos (Two)
Tres (Three)
Cuatro (Four)
Cinco (Five)
Seis (Six)
Siete (Seven)
Ocho (Eight)
Nueve (Nine)
Diez (Ten)

From *Celebration Games: Physical Activities for Every Month,* by Barb Wnek, 2006, Champaign, IL: Human Kinetics.

CINCO DE MAYO HISTORY

Cinco de Mayo means the fifth of May in Spanish. It celebrates the victory of the Mexican army, led by Benito Juarez, over the French. This victory took place on May 5, 1862, in Puebla, a Mexican town. The victory gave Mexico more freedom. On this day, Hispanics dress up, have parades, display fireworks, and eat Mexican food. People all over the United States celebrate with Mexican food, music, and dancing.

From *Celebration Games: Physical Activities for Every Month,* by Barb Wnek, 2006, Champaign, IL: Human Kinetics.

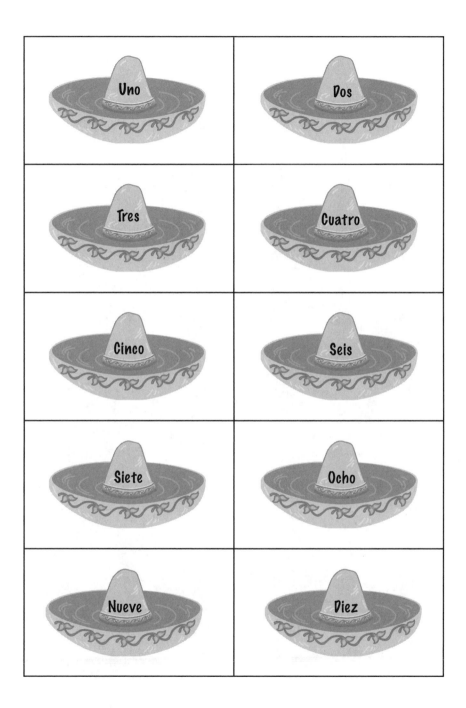

From *Celebration Games: Physical Activities for Every Month,* by Barb Wnek, 2006, Champaign, IL: Human Kinetics.

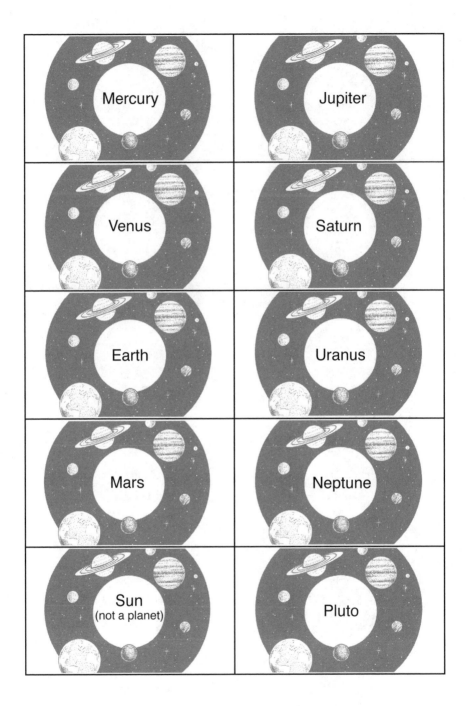

From *Celebration Games: Physical Activities for Every Month,* by Barb Wnek, 2006, Champaign, IL: Human Kinetics.

ABOUT THE AUTHOR

Barb Wnek has been a physical educator for more than 25 years, teaching 3- to 14-year-old students in both public and private school settings. She currently teaches K-6 physical education and health in the Ferguson-Florissant School District in Florissant, Missouri. For nearly two decades, Wnek has also taught physical education to gifted children at the Gifted Resource Council Summer Camps in St. Louis, Missouri.

In 2003, Wnek's teaching approach earned her recognition as one of Dole's nationwide Creative 5 A Day Teacher of the Year awards. She was also selected to be an Olympic torchbearer for the 2004 Summer Olympics because of her accomplishments in motivating students to get active through fun and innovative educational experiences.

Wnek is a member of American Alliance for Health, Physical Education, Recreation and Dance (AAHPERD) and the Missouri Alliance for Health, Physical Education, Recreation and Dance (MOAHPERD). She holds a master's degree along with 30 additional credit hours in physical education and health. In her spare time, Wnek has run more than 35 marathons and has danced on *St. Louis Country,* a country-western and swing dance show, for the past eight years. She resides in Brentwood, Missouri.